PATRICK LUCIANI

What Canadians Believe but Shouldn't About their Economy

26 Economic Myths

Addison-Wesley Publishers

Don Mills, Ontario • Reading, Massachusetts
Menlo Park, California • New York •
Wokingham, England • Amsterdam • Bonn
Sydney • Singapore • Tokyo • Madrid • San Juan

Coordinating Editor: *Heather Rignanesi and Kateri Lanthier*
Designer: *Anthony Leung*
Author photo: *Jeremy Jones*

Canadian Cataloguing in Publication Data
Luciani, Patrick
 What Canadians believe but shouldn't about their economy

ISBN 0-201-60168-0

1. Canada – Economic conditions - 1991 -
2. Canada – Economic policy - 1991 -
I. Title.

HC115.L83 1993   330.971´0647   C92-095730-7

ISBN 0-201-60168-0

Printed and bound in Canada.

A B C D – ALG – 96 95 94 93

"To my father,

who once believed all these myths,

but now believes only some of them"

CONTENTS

PREFACE

How often have we heard arguments like 'the government will go broke before I retire', 'we can't compete with low Mexican wages', 'immigrants steal jobs', 'we need a cheaper dollar' or 'we're loosing manufacturing jobs permanently'? These are only a few of the economic platitudes we hear each day. They've taken on the aura of conventional wisdom, and in a democracy, it's a short step from *public knowledge* to public policy.

One example is rent controls. Economists insist that rent controls hurt the very group they are intended to help. In Toronto, rent controls have virtually stopped all construction of apartment buildings, while in Paris, prospective renters check the obituaries for leads. In New York City, tenants pay more for parking than rent. Yet, whenever there is a housing crunch, politicians turn to rent controls that only make the situation worse. Economic myth battled economic reality during the free trade debate in the late 1980's. Many people clung to the notion of economic independence, as though the international marketplace had not expanded since Sir John A. Macdonald's National Policy of 1878.

Who's to blame for the low level of economic literacy? One culprit is the media that insists on giving both good and bad economic arguments equal weight in an effort to appear impartial. Professional economists in Canada, preferring to keep their discipline in the classroom, also share some of the blame. It is not unusual to find Nobel Prize economists writing in the popular media in America, while in Canada, the best economic thinkers are relatively unknown.

Without some background in economic reasoning, no one can distinguish between arguments that make sense and those that don't. The intention of this book is to dispel some of the common economic myths and to help the general reader think clearly about economic and public policy issues. You may not agree with all the conclusions reached in this book, but reading it will have been worth the effort if you no longer take for granted everything you hear about the economy.

ACKNOWLEDGEMENTS

Even though only my name appears on the cover, books are seldom completed by one person. This project is no exception. With this in mind, I want to thank my editors at Addison-Wesley, Heather Rignanesi, Beth Bruder and especially Shirley Tessier who believed in the book from the beginning and gave me the encouragement to sit down and write it. Special mention has to go to the tireless work of my copy editors Shirley Corriveau and Kateri Lanthier, who succeeded in keeping me on schedule.

Then there are my many friends on College Street who debated policy issues over countless cappuccinos at the Bar Italia, and who convinced me a book like this was not only necessary but essential. Finally, I want to thank my father, who with great restraint and patience, listened to all my arguments but still believes that the government will go broke any day now.

Patrick Luciani
Toronto, Ontario
February 1993

MYTH 1

RENT CONTROLS ARE NEEDED DURING A HOUSING SHORTAGE

nyone who has seen the demolished and abandoned buildings in the Bronx, New York, can't forget the images. The scale of the devastation is overwhelming. Landlords are abandoning two thousand housing units a month while the city has been left with 150,000 derelict units occupied only by rats and small-time cocaine dealers. This damage wasn't caused solely by migration to the suburbs, vandalism or the race riots of the 1970s, but by the attempt to control prices — that is, by rent controls.

It has been said that next to bombing, rent controls can best destroy a city's rental housing. Even if the damage isn't as overwhelming, the perverse effects are just as striking. Wherever rent controls are in force, for example, in London, Paris and Rome, the results are similar; and Canada's big cities aren't immune. Yet a large portion of the population believes the myth that rent controls are needed during a housing shortage, despite the theory and evidence that controls are inefficient and self-defeating.

HOW RENT CONTROLS WORK

Before analyzing the cost of rent controls, here's how they work. Rent control legislation is usually enacted during a time of rapid economic growth when a housing shortage is a problem. Rent controls are a form of price ceiling that freeze or moderate the price increases of rental units. These prices are set below what the market would otherwise allow in the absence of controls. As with a shortage of any commodity, prices go up in the short term until more commodity, in this case more rental housing, can be supplied.

It is important to note that without market interference, a supply shortage can't last forever. Prices will eventually moderate as supply catches up with demand. But rental housing can't be brought on stream overnight. With some products that can react to short-ages quickly, prices hardly change. For example, if there's a shortage of ice cream during the summer, the manufacturer simply increases production without any effect on prices. Housing, on the other hand, takes time. There are investors to find, building permits to arrange, and contractors to hire. In the meantime, the need for more housing increases while the supply stays constant. If the economy experiences inflationary pressures, as happened in 1975 when Ontario introduced rent controls, rents start rising rapidly.[1] Moreover, when the price of housing goes up too quickly, pressure builds on politicians to do something about it.

POLITICAL REASONS FOR RENT CONTROLS

Governments don't normally step in to stop prices from rising. The price of cars, for example, becomes whatever the market will bear. Housing, however, is considered an essential commodity and because of that is treated differently. Rent controls are introduced for a number of explicit or implicit reasons. Explicitly, governments want to be perceived as helpers of the poor, seniors and other groups on fixed incomes who are vulnerable to rent hikes. It's polit-ically unsavoury to allow images (whether accurate or not) of unscrupulous landlords taking advantage of people or making windfall gains at the expense of the disadvantaged.

Implicitly, governments see rent controls as a form of redis-tributing income from the rich to the poor. Although rarely stated that bluntly, keeping rents down is thought to be a form of subsidiz-ing the income of the poor.

Another reason for rent controls is that they are expedient in the short run — that is, politicians get credit for solving a perceived problem quickly. Also, let's not forget raw politics. Rental dwellers make up a sizeable group of any major city's population. In Metropolitan Toronto, for example, renters account for 42 percent of all households. The political power of the Metro Tenants Association is such that no political party in Ontario advocates eliminating rent controls. They are an identifiable group that can bring considerable political pressure to bear on government and, as such, are beneficiaries. The victims, on the other hand, are those who will need housing in the future and will have to deal with shortages. Obviously, this unidentifiable group has no political power — the cruel irony being that those most hurt by controls believe that controls are a benefit rather than a problem.

Such is the distortion of misguided government policies. As with most economic policies, nothing is free. Rent controls are no exception. In this case, not only are they expensive for society and completely inadequate in meeting the needs of the poor, but they have been a public policy disaster in every city where they have been introduced.

ECONOMIC CONSEQUENCES OF RENT CONTROLS

Economic theory shows us that any form of price controls create effects that are at once apparent and far-reaching — price controls create shortages. With rent control, the results are somewhat subtle but nonetheless important.

The reasons for control-induced shortages are simple. At artificially low prices, or price ceilings, more of a commodity will be demanded but with price restrictions, the market can't respond to fill the need. Governments have removed the most important incentive to do so — profit. Once profits are removed, or lowered, by holding down prices, supply will always be less than demand (see Figure 1.1). If supply is constant or shrinking as demand increases, something has to give. In this case, it's a continuing shortage of rental housing. It's that simple. That alone is bad enough, but the story doesn't end there.

If landlords can't make a suitable return on their investment, they start taking existing units off the market for other more profitable uses. Apartments are converted to condominiums, shopping malls, or even parking lots.[2] Governments then set up expensive regulations and bureaucracies to prevent landlords from converting their units. In response, landlords go through a lot of trouble circumventing new laws and legislation, which in turn wastes their own and society's resources. Ontario currently spends over $30 million annually on regulating rent controls, money that would be better spent helping the poor.

Builders and landlords can't be blamed for the housing shortage. They are only responding to the incentives (or lack of them), created by government policy. Apartments are needed, but they are not being built by private business because there is no profit to be made. Instead a surplus of expensive condominiums sit empty, while the need for affordable rental units grows.[3]

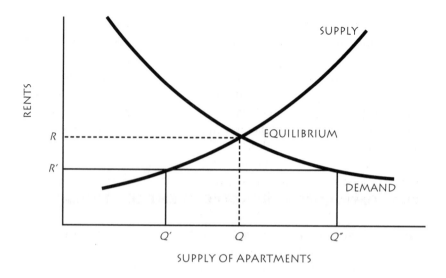

SUPPLY

RENTS

R - EQUILIBRIUM

R'

DEMAND

Q'   Q   Q"

SUPPLY OF APARTMENTS

NOTE: The market for rental apartments is in equilibrium when rents are at *R*. At *R'* the number of units for rent is *Q*. If rents are held down at *R'* by rent controls, the rental price ceiling, the number of units provided by the free market falls to *Q'*, but the demand at this lower rent is *Q"* leading to an excess demand for apartment units and a chronic shortage.

FIGURE 1.1   HOW RENT CONTROLS REDUCE THE SUPPLY OF APARTMENTS

If a landlord can't tear a building down, build a mall, or convert existing premises to condominiums, the only alternative left, if existing rents aren't sufficient to cover rising costs, is to allow the building to deteriorate. After all, governments freeze rents, not the costs of upkeep. Here we have the worst of all possible scenarios: a shrinking supply of rental units, a growing wasteful bureaucracy that pits landlord against tenant, and rundown buildings.[4] In the final analysis, the burden of providing new affordable housing falls on the shoulders of government — in other words, the taxpayer. Before rent controls were introduced in Ontario, the provincial government helped subsidize 27 percent of all rental units. By 1985, it was over 75 percent. Ontario's Home Now program has allocated $3 billion in capital costs and $300 million in operating subsidies to build 30,000 nonprofit and co-op units to meet a chronic housing need that could have been filled by the private sector if it had not been for rent controls.

But the problem is not handled yet. As the shortage worsens, a black market for apartments develops as substandard units come on the market at prices higher than allowed by the controls. People have to live somewhere, so they aren't anxious to complain if they are overcharged or their accommodations don't meet municipal standards. Many tenants are happy just to have a place to stay.

More obvious abuses are things such as landlords demanding key money as a form of rent increase. Although illegal, this practice is widespread during a housing shortage. There is also the waste of time and resources in looking for a place to live. In some cities, such as Rome and Paris, the shortage is so acute that people inherit apartments from one generation to the next. It's not unknown for apartment hunters to track the obituary columns to see if a unit has been vacated because of a death. The situation is so out of hand in New York City that rent controls create the anomaly where some people pay more for their parking spaces, which are unregulated, than they do for rent.

What about the poor and low income families this legislation was supposed to help? How are they faring through all of this? There's no denying that there are some winners. They were the ones lucky enough to be in an apartment before the controls were enacted — and many of them were in need of help. But the poor aren't the only ones who rent. Those who could afford to pay higher rents are now being subsidized by those who can't find proper accommodation. Rent controls have the effect of trading off the benefits of those lucky enough to be living in rent controlled buildings at the time the legislation was passed at the expense of those looking for accommodation at a later date.

Studies have found that the bulk of the benefits do not go to low-income rental dwellers. It's not uncommon, for example, to find a single mother paying $800 a month for a basement apartment in Toronto while a six-figure executive lives in a $600 a month rent-controlled apartment. Thirty percent of Ontario's subsidized housing will go to those who can afford to pay market rents. Over 70 percent of those earning over $60,000 a year spend less than 20 percent of their income on rents, whereas 53 percent of those earning below $25,000 have to spend over 30 percent.[5] Often those in the upper income bracket hold onto rent controlled units while investing in real estate. In this case, taxpayers are subsidizing the rich to further help build their equity base at the expense of the poor.

The tragedy of rent controls is that politicians know the damage this type of legislation can do, but they can't seem to avoid the temptation of a temporary solution to a long-term problem.

Economists can't tell the decision makers what to do, but they can make them aware of the consequences of their actions. The adverse effects of rent controls are well documented.[6]

SOLUTIONS WITHOUT THE SIDE-EFFECTS

The obvious question to ask at this stage is: Is there a better way? Can we house the poor and low income families at a lower cost to society? The answer is yes.

Economists are a stingy lot by profession. They want to know the least expensive way to reach society's objectives (in this case properly housing low income groups and the poor) without wasting resources. A better way is to allow the market to make decisions about where resources should be allocated. In other words, investors normally go where the returns are the highest. One solution is to eliminate rent controls and replace it with a voucher system, which would subsidize the poor directly with vouchers, or rent supplements that could be redeemed for cash by landlords. How much each family or individual received in vouchers would be determined by an income or means test. A simple voucher system would allow the market to increase rental housing, moderate rents in the short term and long term by improving profitability, and help those who need it most — the poor. To those who object to a means test, it should be pointed out that they are already in place and working for those who collect welfare and unemployment insurance. Besides, vouchers are preferable to waiting in line at a food bank because all your money has gone to pay the rent. However, one thing is clear: there's no free lunch. Whether through rent controls, government subsidized housing, or direct help to the poor with vouchers, someone pays.

Although more expensive in the beginning, the voucher system is cheaper and more efficient in the long run for society because it leaves intact the incentives to private investors to supply more rental accommodation; it doesn't require as expensive a bureaucracy to administer; and it helps the poor without subsidizing those that don't need it.

If a solution is known, why is there no action? The answer is that once vested interests are entrenched, it's difficult to dislodge them. Those who gain from rent controls — those who now live in rent-controlled buildings — have an interest in keeping their rents below market values. Moreover, as long as vested interests hold the ear of politicians, the situation worsens. The best time to get rid of rent controls is during a period of slow growth and moderate inflation when the cost of housing is at its lowest. After that, it's a question of political will.

NOTES

[1] In the late seventies, rent controls were in effect in every province in Canada. In 1979, they were partially removed in British Columbia, Alberta and Saskatchewan, but reintroduced or extended in New Brunswick, Manitoba and Ontario.

[2] Anyone who wants a better idea of rent control waste should read W.T. Standbury and John D. Todd, "Landlords as Economic Prisoners of War," in *Canadian Public Policy*, fall 1990, pp. 399–417.

[3] With rent controls, the vacancy rate in Toronto has fallen to 0.2 percent. In other words, there were only 565 free units in a rental market of 282,668 units in 1990. By 1991, the vacancy rate rose to around 2 percent for the first time since 1972. But the higher vacancy rates and falling rents were a consequence of the recession and not of rent controls. In such a case no one would recommend that landlords be protected with controls to stop rents from falling.

[4] In some cases rent controls have made tenants better off than their landlords, especially small investors who have put their savings into small apartment buildings only to find they cannot keep them up or recover costs.

[5] Eliot Research, 1989 Metro Toronto survey as found in the *Annual Report 1989* of the Fair Rental Policy Organization of Ontario, p.4. George Fallis and Lawrence Smith give a good account of how the poor are affected by controls in their paper, "Rent Control in Toronto: Tenant Rationing and Tenant Benefits," in *Canadian Public Policy*, summer 1985.

[6] A valuable source of information is the report based on a study commissioned by the Ontario government and headed by Stuart Thom, entitled *Report of the Commission of Inquiry into Residential Tenancies* (Toronto: Ontario Ministry of the Attorney General, 1987), April 1987.

MYTH 2

PAY EQUITY SHOULD BE BACKED BY LAW

anadian women earn less than men. This comes as no surprise to women who, on average, earn two-thirds of what men earn, ignoring occupational differences. Traditionally, women have been paid lower wages for doing the same kinds of work and have been concentrated in lower-paying jobs. This is a situation women are no longer willing to tolerate. Gone are the days when women passively accept wages and earnings less than they deserve. This trend towards equalization has become stronger as women enter the labour force in greater numbers and go into professions and occupations once dominated by men.

If women cannot satisfy their wage demands in the marketplace, they are determined to get them through legislation.[1] To get rid of the wage difference between the sexes, women are advocating not only that they want *equal pay for equal work*, but *equal pay for work of equal value*.[2] Women argue that it is not enough to earn the same wage or salary as men within occupations, but that they must do so between occupations as well if justice in the workplace is to prevail. There is no reason why male janitors should earn more than female office cleaners when they both do essentially the same work. But what are the costs of passing such laws for employers, women and society at large? Is legislation the best way to guarantee that women are properly compensated for their work? Or is the most effective option to guarantee that women have equal opportunity in education and employment and leave the market to set wages? Let's examine the issue more closely to see which method makes more sense.

THE PROBLEM

When it comes to wage rates, there are two schools of thought. The first view holds that wages in a free market are set by what economists call the marginal revenue product (MRP) of labour. In other words, wages are set according to the productivity and direct value of labour. The more productive the labour, the more value it is to the employer, and the higher the wages. In a market where the employer doesn't discriminate between male or female workers, there is no reason that wages should be different for either sex. What an employer pays is based on a whole range of criteria, such as education, experience, working conditions, occupational mobility and so on. If female wages are lower, it's because the market, for whatever reason, values the work of women less than men. A second view says that women's choices are not free and that wage differences cannot be explained by productivity differences alone. Because of social discrimination women are channelled into less-productive and therefore lower-paying jobs. This second position has some merit. Even when productive characteristics, such as education, skills and experience are taken into consideration along with the fact that women are segregated into lower-paying occupational groups, there still remains about a 10 to 15 percent wage difference that can only be explained by sex discrimination.[3] It is that differential that legislation is geared to eliminate. Since the market can not do the job of equalizing wages and salaries, goes the argument, then legislation is needed to correct the imbalance.[4]

One way is by introducing laws that compel employers to pay their workers the same wages and salaries not only for identical jobs, but also for jobs of equal value. "Equal pay for work of equal value" or pay equity legislation is interested more in compensating women where occupational segregation caused by the socialization of women at early ages has forced them into certain job categories. This, then, introduces a new problem into the equation. Who determines the definition of "jobs of equal value"? Outside agencies now must determine how to evaluate jobs where there is no comparable job done by men. This may seem like a small hurdle to overcome by someone who favours such legislation, but the costs of implementing equal value laws may not be as trivial as first assumed. A whole new bureaucracy is needed just to evaluate the differences and similarities between occupations. It's one thing to say women and men should be paid the same for jobs that are the same; but how are jobs to be compared that are not related? In order to evaluate two totally different jobs, pay equity legislation relies on a point system assigned to various criteria, such as skills, effort, experience, responsibility and working conditions. These points are added up to see which jobs are comparable and then wages are based accordingly.

For example, in the case of hospitals, what jobs are comparable with nursing — physicians or stationary engineers working in the boiler rooms? In the end all evaluation techniques are fundamentally arbitrary and can at best only estimate the value between one job and another. This task is difficult enough in large firms where there are a number of jobs that can be compared — for instance, a female-dominated job such as a clerical supervisor and a male-dominated job in shipping. But what about small firms where job categories or responsibilities are not that clearly drawn? Some have argued that the adminstration costs don't have to be permanent and that the equal value laws can be used to change the perceptions of employers about undervaluing the work of women. Experience shows, however, that rules and regulations once imposed are tough to dislodge.

WHO PAYS?

As with any government policy that entails setting prices, there are winners and losers. Equal pay for work of equal value legislation is no exception. The winners are those women who will benefit from the legislation with higher wages. Society might benefit from the increased job satisfaction and productivity of these women. However, these benefits do not come without costs.

First are the costs that economists attribute to the misallocation of resources, or allocative inefficiencies. What this means is that even if two jobs require the same skills, education and experience, the market still might pay one more than the other. One job might be riskier (for example, welding), while the other may be more popular and attract more people (for example, acting). On average welders earn more than actors, but their salary difference can be explained by factors other than skills and experience. The reason the two jobs pay differently is that the market knows that to entice workers to go into welding, usually a tough, dirty and cyclically unstable job, they have to pay more not only in absolute terms, but also in relation to other jobs as well. If wages for actors are increased, more people will want to go into the theatre and fewer into welding. Those hiring welders will now have to pay higher wages to attract the necessary number of workers and increase the costs of products which they produce. Unemployment will increase among actors as more are now willing to work at the higher wage. In short, we now have a situation of too many actors and not enough welders.[5] Governments can set the wages of a certain profession, but they cannot compel employers to hire all those who want to work at those new and higher wages. No one can measure the costs in terms of the misallocation of resources, but no one can deny that they exist and are substantial.

Another allocative cost to society caused by pay equity is the cost of stifling mobility between occupations by changes in supply and demand. If the pay for engineers, for example, goes up because of an increase in demand for their services, relative to college professors, this acts as a market signal that there is a shortage of engineers. If those signals are concealed because pay equity arbitrarily erases the wage differences between these occupations, then society loses crucial mobility and flexibility when economic conditions change.

Second are the added expenses to the employer of the entire program. One study estimates the cost at between $2,200 and $3,300 (in 1986 dollars) for every worker to close the wage gap by 10 percent between men and women.[6] Companies that have to implement equal pay legislation are concerned about the effects of higher costs on their businesses. Most programs allow for some form of program phase-in over a period of time, but that doesn't alleviate the problem that someone, either the firm or the customer, has to pay. These costs are exclusive of the millions of dollars paid by taxpayers to set up commissions to monitor and administer the program.[7] Although equal value implicitly allows for the increase in wage for females in certain jobs, and a decrease in wage in other male-dominated ones, few if any government agencies or private companies will reduce wages paid to men who may be identified as overpaid.[8] That is one reason employers are so opposed to the legislation.

Finally there is the cost to women themselves. In any form of government control that tries to regulate prices either by setting a floor price, as in minimum wages, or ceiling prices, as in rent controls, someone pays, and it's usually those the legislation was intended to help. Laws to correct a wage difference are no exception. If the wages of women are increased, then fewer women will be hired regardless of whether or not sexual discrimination existed in the first place. As already mentioned, some women will benefit from higher wages, at the costs of others losing theirs.[9] These factors do not take into consideration that more expensive female labour may be substituted with more capital, or that men may now compete for the higher-paying jobs in the sectors once dominated by women.[10] Pay equity laws cannot by themselves eliminate wage differentials without costs. As with any policy to compensate one group over another by interfering with the market, the benefits do not come free.

IS THERE A BETTER SOLUTION?

If economics tells us that equal pay for work of equal value legislation comes only at a price for society in terms of less-efficient use of resources and higher unemployment of women, how can the wage differential be eliminated? As with most government policies that try to improve the lot of one group over another, there are no short-term or easy answers. In the case of equal pay, the most effective

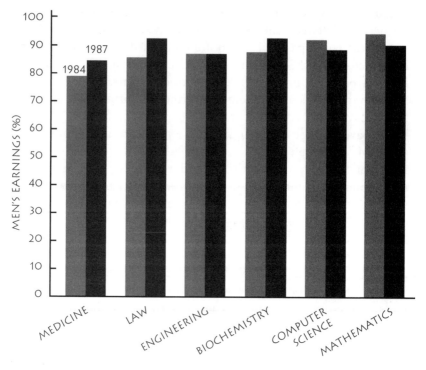

WOMEN'S EARNINGS (1984, 1987)

NOTE: Based on 1984 salaries.

Source: StatsCan, Perspectives, summer 1990.

FIGURE 2.1   WAGE GAP SHRINKS WITH MORE EDUCATION

means to increasing women's earning potential is to encourage them to go into jobs and occupations that pay higher wages, and that means going into jobs dominated by men. Here education and training are key.

One federal government study showed that the earning gap between full-time male and female university graduates was 82 percent in 1987 compared to 70 percent for the entire work force.[11] A portion of the difference in wages could be explained by the fact that men tended to go into the higher-paying professions, such as engineering, medicine and computer sciences, while women went into the lower-paying jobs in education and the humanities. But how did women do within the various professions? Unfortunately a gap still persists, but it is shrinking. By taking into consideration the field of study and level of education, the study estimated that women earned about 92 percent of the male salary in 1987.[12] The conclusion seems to be that the more education women get, the higher their earnings in relation to men (see Figure 2.1). The message seems to be getting through. In the early 1960s only a quarter

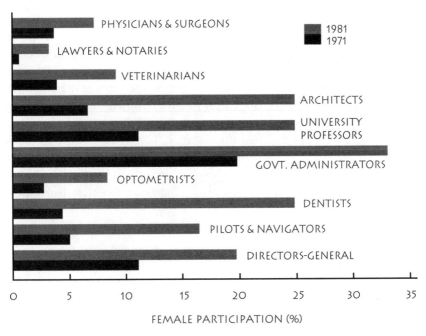

Sources: Economic Council of Canada, On The Mend. Twentieth Annual Review, 1983, Table 5.5.

FIGURE 2.2   NUMBER OF WOMEN WITH HIGH-PAYING JOBS

of undergraduates were women; today they receive more than half of all undergraduate degrees. In fact there has been a dramatic increase in the proportion of degrees earned by women. From the early 1970s to the mid 1980s, the proportion of women graduating in pharmacy went from 38 percent to 62 percent. As well, women showed particular strength in other nontraditional fields as engineering, law, dentistry, agriculture and veterinary medicine (see Figure 2.2). The overall number of degrees granted to women between those same years increased 80 percent compared to 6 percent for men. Women who crossed over to nontraditional jobs earned more and were more likely to work full-time.[13]

Over the next generation, the wage gap between university-educated men and women should narrow even further. Given this trend, it appears that equal pay legislation will have little effect on women with higher levels of training and education and that society should channel its resources to encouraging women to get the education they need to enter job areas once dominated by men. It is occupational segregation of women that accounts for more of the earnings gap than does outright discrimination.[14] In that case, then, women need more employment opportunity rather than equal pay for work of equal value policies.

It seems that pay equity may be treating the symptom rather than the cause of wage discrimination. The problem starts outside the labour market before women enter the labour force. Policies should be directed not at employers, but at the source; there should be greater employment opportunities for women and attempts to change the attitudes of parents, teachers and boys and girls about proper occupations for men and women. Changing children's ideas before they enter the labour force is crucial to changing market behaviour. A radical change is needed in cultural values and attitudes towards women. Without these changes, pay equity legislation won't do women much good.[15]

NOTES

1   Twelve of Canada's jurisdictions have implemented some form of pay equity program. Canadian governments are no longer relying on complaints or evidence of discrimination to increase female wages.

2   Equal pay for work of equal value is interchangeable with the terms "pay equity" and "comparable worth."

3   R.E. Robb, "Equal Pay for Work of Equal Value: Issues and Policies," Canadian Public Policy XIII, 4, winter 1987, pp. 445–61. The wage differential is based on full-time employment. These studies were also based on census data from 1971 and 1981. Legislation for equal pay for work of equal value was introduced at the federal level in 1978, Manitoba in 1976, Quebec in 1978, and Ontario in 1987.

4   It has been argued that there is no real wage gap between men and women that cannot be explained by factors other than sex discrimination. If a true wage differential exists between men and women based solely on sex discrimination and not on ability, then a sharp employer would exploit that difference and hire more women and less men. It is no different for a broker to deal in the arbitrage of an undervalued bond, currency or stock. The question is, why hasn't this happened in the labour market?

5   Productivity drops because of a well-known law in economic theory called the "law of diminishing marginal returns." As the supply of labour increases, the contribution to total output of the last worker drops given that other factors of production (e.g., machinery) are held constant.

6   Robb, "Equal Pay for Work of Equal Value," p. 453.

7   The Canadian Federation of Independent Business estimates that the administration costs for large firms could be as high as $500 per worker, and $300 per worker for small firms.

8   Problems can arise in certain cases where municipal governments may be compelled to raise the salaries in certain jobs. If budgets won't allow them to raise taxes, either services or staff have to be cut in the higher-wage category.

9   In the article by Robb (see note 3), she states that from the preliminary studies based on U.S. Census data, a wage adjustment of 20 percentage points in the public sector will lead to a 2 to 3 percent decline in female employment. The results in the private sector would likely be larger because the wage gap is wider. Given that employment in the private sector is also more "elastic," that is, the demand for labour is more sensitive to wage increases, any increase in female wages would lead to even higher unemployment.

10 In the mid 1970s Australia adopted an equal pay for equal work law. As a result women's wages went from 65 to 93 percent of men's wages from 1970 to 1980. What were the impacts on women's employment? One study found that pay equalization slowed the growth of women's employment by one-third, and increased unemployment by 0.5 percent.

11 Ted Wannell, "Male–female earnings gap among recent university graduates," Perspectives on Labour and Income (Ottawa: Statistics Canada, summer 1990), pp. 19–27.

12 The Wannell study found that for Ph.D. graduates, the wage differential between men and women was virtually nonexistent. In certain occupations there was little wage difference in 1987 for law (5 percent), sociology/anthropology (3 percent), political science (0 percent), biochemistry/biology (5 percent), and mathematics (7 percent). Nevertheless, there remains an unexplained differential in wages

regardless of education and profession. One possible explanation can be found by "statistical discrimination." This means that some employers prefer hiring men because women tend to interrupt their working careers for marriage and children. In the higher occupational categories, this seems less of a factor.

[13] Karen Hughs, "Trading places: Men and women in non-traditional occupations 1971–86," Perspectives on Labour and Income (Ottawa: Statistics Canada, summer 1990). This is consistent with evidence in the U.S., where women were closing the wage gap with men in the 1980s. One reason for this change is that women are getting the education they need. Source: Sylvia Nasar, "Women's Progress Stalled? Not So". The New York Times, Oct. 18, 1992, p. 1, section 3.

[14] That was a major conclusion of Professor Morley Gunderson in his study "Male–Female Wage Differentials and Policy Responses," Journal of Economic Literature, vol. XXVII, March 1989, p.67.

[15] That has been the experience in Australia where they have had pay equity since the early 1970s.

THE FAMILY FARM SHOULD BE PRESERVED AS A WAY OF LIFE

ew things engender such emotional attachment as the notion of preserving the values, traditions and history of Canada's agricultural environment. To protect this way of life, governments have historically intervened to protect the interests of farming regardless of the cost to taxpayers and the consumer. Even though the economic circumstances surrounding agriculture have changed, the myth persists that farming is different from other industries and must be protected come what may.

As with any public policy that distorts free market prices, someone pays the bill. In regards to agriculture, there is no exception. How much do we pay to preserve the family farm and a system of income support for our farmers? The answer is, plenty. In 1990, taxpayers supported the Canadian farmer in the amount of $7.5 billion dollars through direct assistance alone. In addition, consumers had to pay $3.5 billion in higher food costs. That translates into $115,000 for every job saved in agriculture compared to $13,000 to $20,000 in the United States.[1] Despite federal cut-backs in the 1980s to trim the deficit, spending on farm support continued to climb. Farmers now get about half of their income from government support programs (see Figure 3.1). Yet the more governments give farmers, the worse off they are. Of Canada's 280,000 farms, 98 percent are family farms, and 23 percent of these are in financial trouble without any relief in sight. In the last StatsCanada census, 118,400 of all farms in Canada had gross incomes under $50,000. The current farm problem is so large that it may be beyond the fiscal capacity of the government to solve with subsidies and public aid.

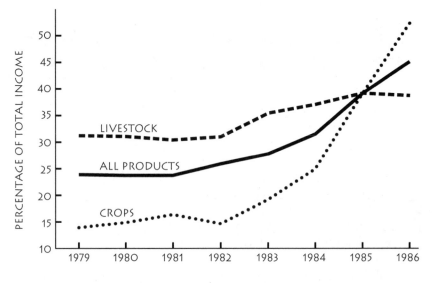

* Producer Subsidy Equivalents (PSE)

Sources: J.C. Gilson, World Agricultural Changes (Toronto: C.D. Howe Institute, 1989);
OECD, Monitoring and Outlook of Agricultural Policies, Markets and Trade
(Paris, May 1988).

FIGURE 3.1 PERCENTAGE OF FARM INCOME FROM GOVERNMENT SUBSIDIES*

What happened to farm policy in Canada that seemed to make
everyone worse off including the taxpayer, consumer and farmer? A
good part of the answer lies in how governments get involved in
supporting farmers, not only in Canada but around the world.

WHY AND HOW GOVERNMENTS GET INVOLVED

Government has always been interested in securing adequate sup-
plies of food for its citizens. On that basis alone it has been considered in the best interest of a country to intervene in agricultural production by protecting domestic farmers from imports. A nation's
dignity has been defined by its ability to feed itself and become self-
sufficient. In line with this, another reason for involvement has to
do with securing farm incomes. It has long been known that in agriculture incomes can fluctuate wildly from year to year caused mainly by large shifts in supply. Weather conditions, for example, have a

MYTH 3 — THE FAMILY FARM SHOULD BE PRESERVED AS A WAY OF LIFE lot to do with how much wheat, corn or fruit is harvested. Bumper crops tend to depress prices, while crop shortages push them up. It is one of the ironies in agriculture that good harvests don't always coincide with good incomes. Agricultural commodity prices are very sensitive to small changes in supply and this is one of the strongest justifications for government intervention — the stabilization of farm prices and incomes. Finally there's the practical matter that farmers have traditionally carried a lot of political clout, and for that reason alone demand special attention.

There are a number of ways governments intervene in agricultural markets. The Americans and the French, for example, prefer to provide price support programs in which they buy, at a fair market price above that dictated by supply and demand, as much as the farmer can produce. The farmer now has the incentive to increase profit and income by producing as much as possible. At these artificially higher prices, or floor prices, farmers farm more intensively to raise yields. But there's a catch — in order for governments to maintain these higher prices, less is demanded by consumers. The governments now have the added expense of storing this excess production, or selling it in international markets at below the cost of production. In the United States, taxpayers pay the cost of buying the produce in the first place, plus the added cost of literally paying farmers millions of dollars not to produce.[2] Price support programs are so out of hand in the United States that by the late 1980s there was enough grain in storage to make seven loaves of bread for every man, woman, and child on Earth! At the same time there is a shortage of oats because the price supports for wheat are so much higher. European farmers have also become rich under their Common Agricultural Policy where farmers sell to the state as much as they can at prices above those set by the market.

MARKETING BOARDS

Canadians have chosen another way to help their farmers. For seasonal crops such as fruits and vegetables the government provides straight subsidies and tariff protection. But for the big cash crops such as grain and dairy products, governments use that uniquely Canadian institution, marketing boards.

In the case of grain and oilseed where the bulk of production is exported, the Canadian government acts as the selling agent for the farmer. The most famous of this type is the Canadian Wheat Marketing Board, which pays the wheat farmer 75 percent of the world price and then sells the wheat on behalf of the farmer. When the wheat is sold, the farmers get the difference. In the event that prices on the world markets collapse below the original 75 percent level between the time the government buys and sells the wheat, the loss is absorbed by the federal treasury. By providing 75 percent of the estimated average selling price over the year, the government assures that farmers do not have to worry about short-term fluctuations in price and can be assured of a set price at time of delivery.[3]

Marketing boards for dairy, poultry and eggs work differently. Their objective is to control the price of these commodities by restricting their supply with quotas. Without a quota, a farmer can not sell his or her produce. Quotas control how much is produced, which in turn determines the price. If prices are stabilized, so are incomes for farmers. National quotas for Canada's supply-managed commodities are aimed at making the country self-sufficient but are enforced with strict controls on imports and foreign competition. Only by buying an existing quota can someone get into farming in those areas controlled by supply-managed marketing boards; and the price of quotas do not come cheaply. The price of the quota reflects the value of the profits or income generated by the restricted supply.[4] The higher the profits in, say, the production of eggs, the higher the cost of purchasing a quota. It is not surprising that the entire system is popular among farmers who hold quotas because it guarantees them a stabilized income above what they could get in a free market.[5]

WHAT WENT WRONG

In the case of grain marketing boards, everything works well when world prices are either steady or going up. That is what happened in the early 1970s when world grain prices went from $70 per tonne to over $200 per tonne when grain shortages began to appear around the world. Along with the rise in grain prices the cost of farmland went up, averaging 15 percent to 20 percent increases. Farmers who were "just getting by" a few years before, were now borrowing heavily and growing rich overnight (on paper at least). By 1981 farm property values topped $103 billion, two-and-a-half times their value of a decade earlier and much of it supported by farm debt that banks were more than willing to provide. Then things slowly began to sour.

Farmers reacted as anyone would when prices go up. They bought more land and brought it into production, but a lot of this land was marginal, which meant higher costs of production. But that didn't seem to matter as long as the price of wheat kept rising. Farmers were also investing more in high-yield, disease and drought resistant crops, which helped yields more than double in North America from 1965 to 1980. However, these developments were taking place everywhere; and countries we once exported to were becoming self-sufficient themselves. World grain production was steadily increasing — this was bad news for Canadian grain farmers who were mortgaged to the hilt when the inevitable price collapse finally occurred. What followed was traumatic: European and American wheat producers started competing madly for a shrinking world market. By 1987, grain farmers were getting $60 per tonne where they had gotten $186 just a few years before. The real price for Canadian wheat in 1986 was less than 50 percent of that received during the depression. Despite the price increases in the early 1970s, the long-term trend for wheat prices was down.[6] Canadian farmers had gambled and lost.

Grain farming was a victim of its own success. Better farming techniques and advances in genetic engineering and biotechnology increased yields to the point where farm production in developed countries have more than kept pace with world population growth. Canada produces 70 percent more grain than it needs to be self-sufficient, compared to Japan, which only produces slightly more than half of its national food requirements.

Ottawa's high interest rate policy in the early 1980s did not help matters. Farmers were struggling to hold on as land values dropped and equity disappeared. As if that wasn't enough, the droughts in the Prairies made a bad situation worse. All Ottawa could do was wait for better times and hand out more subsidies. In the end the federal government and taxpayer were victims of poor planning, cutthroat international marketing and bad luck. The irony is that the Canadian government is forced to help perhaps the most efficient producers in the world mainly because countries such as the United States insist on subsidizing their farmers with trade-distorting price support programs.

Where grain producers have no control over world prices, marketing boards for dairy, eggs and poultry are designed to get back that control from the vagaries of supply and demand. But where the costs are obvious to everyone, as is the case in grain subsidies, the support for supply management programs is more subtle but just as damaging.

As with any scheme by governments to stabilize incomes by restricting supply, the consumer pays a price higher than would exist under a free market and consumes a quantity less than dictated by the free market.[7] It's not surprising that Canadians pay 20 percent more for their chickens and eggs. Even food producers are compelled to buy their inputs from marketing boards, thus raising the cost for consumers. Perhaps more important, however, is the fact that marketing boards distort production efficiency and actually reward the least efficient producer. Once a farmer has a quota, there is little or no incentive to compete and cut production costs. The younger more efficient farmer also pays a price because many find the cost of quotas prohibitive. Chicken quotas are about $30 a bird, which means that anyone who wants to buy a modest six-thousand- chicken farm would need $180,000, and that is even before taking into consideration land and capital equipment. Anyone lucky enough to have a quota from when they were being given out tends to hang on to it as long as possible resulting in too many small inefficient producers. Canada had 1,776 egg producers in 1987 compared to the 2,000 in the United States that served a market ten times as large.

Not all farmers benefit equally from supply management. Of the forty thousand poultry, egg and dairy producers, or approximately 14 percent of Canada's farms, they account for 21 percent of the cash receipts in Canada, or $4.2 billion in 1986. Most of that went to the farmers in Quebec and Ontario, who have considerable political clout. Those two provinces hold 80 percent of the industrial milk quota, 55 percent of the egg quota, 68 percent of the turkey quota and 66 percent of the chicken quota. Wheat producers get 50 percent of their entire incomes from taxpayers, while dairy farmers receive over 80 percent of their incomes from higher prices paid by consumers through supply management programs. It's understandable therefore that Ontario and Quebec farmers are strong defenders of supply management. Farmers protected by marketing boards argue that these costs are worth paying because extra taxes are not needed to prop up farm incomes. That's true, but higher prices hit the poorer consumer more than the rich given that the poor spend a higher proportion of their income on food. Taxes on the other had are more equitable if they are progressive and more open to scrutiny by taxpayers.

The ultimate irony is that despite decades of protecting the family farm with massive transfers of money and income support systems, the farmer is under growing pressure just to survive. The entire system worked well when prices and demand for food products generally moved upward. But in periods of prolonged price declines, overproduction, and greater international competition, the economy is left burdened with overcapacity, an inefficient network of trade-distorting income support programs, and the prospect of greater shifts in income to the farm sector. Although marketing boards protect jobs in farming, thousands of potential jobs are lost in food processing because of the higher costs of production.

THE IMPACT OF REMOVING SUPPORT PROGRAMS

What would happen if we simply got rid of all the subsidies and programs that stabilize farm incomes? How much production would be lost in Canada from farms going out of business? One estimate says that farm output would drop by 16.7 percent compared to 13.6 percent for all Organization for Economic Co-operation and Development (OECD) countries if they in turn did the same thing. But because taxes from the industrial and service sectors would fall, nonfarm output in Canada would increase by 0.9 percent, and real household incomes would also go up by 1.3 percent.[8]

Another concern is that prices would climb if we got rid of the subsidies. Perhaps some would climb, but not by much. In many cases, such as poultry, eggs and cheese, they would come down. There is an abundance of world agricultural production that would keep farm prices low. Canadians could take advantage of lower food prices from U.S. producers. (Canadians living close to the United States already take advantage of lower food costs by shopping south of the border where dairy, eggs and poultry prices are considerably lower than in Canada.) But if we got rid of the subsidies, consider what Canadians could do with the billions saved on propping up farms that have little or no prospects for competing in a more competitive world. That kind of money could pay for a lot of schools, hospitals and day care facilities. Realistically, such dramatic changes in income transfers to the agricultural sector are not about to happen any time soon, but world pressures are clearly moving away from guaranteed income support for farmers and towards a system of greater market-oriented trade.[9]

HARD CHOICES AHEAD

The government now faces a dilemma: whether to sacrifice one group of farmers to save another. The radical cry from some farm groups that not one farm should be allowed to go under simply is not feasible. If Canada wants greater access to world grain markets it cannot argue for import restrictions to help dairy farmers. Eventually taxpayers and consumers simply will refuse to carry the growing burden of agricultural income support programs. Food manufacturers have been warning governments and farmers that billions of dollars of investment would be lost if ways are not found to get product costs down. Governments cannot indefinitely justify bailing out farmers while they allow other small businesses to go bankrupt.[10]

In the end the choice may be out of the hands of the federal government as pressure builds in the General Agreement on Tariffs and Trade (GATT) to reduce agricultural trade restrictions worldwide. GATT has already put Canada on notice that they won't allow our supply management programs to exist if we hope to gain greater access to foreign markets.[11] Canada supported the United States in their motion at GATT calling for the removal of all trade-distorting subsidies. Although the federal government has gone on record supporting supply management, it seems unlikely they would go to the wall to defend them indefinitely given Canada's support for trade liberalization in general. The successful farms of the future will be those that can compete internationally. The transition to freer markets for agriculture won't be easy, but the days of keeping farming and the family farm going at any cost are at an end.

NOTES

[1] OECD estimates as reported in *The Financial Post* (9 April 1990), adapted from Michael Parkin and Robin Bade, *Economics* (Don Mills: Addison-Wesley, 1991).

[2] In the United States about 78 million acres, an area the size of New Mexico, are covered by acreage-restriction programs. Farmers often get around these restrictions by increasing yields on available land.

[3] Federal marketing boards are not the only way farmers get assistance. In light of the droughts in the late 1980s billions of dollars went to grain farmers in an

array of subsidies covering transportation, insurance, irrigation and bail-outs. Farmers also got lump-sum payments when world prices collapsed as they did in the late 1980s and early 1990s.

4 Canada is close to being self-sufficient in most agricultural products including those products covered by supply-managed commodities. Although there are some provisions for marginal imports (e.g., some cheeses), it's vital that competition by foreign producers be strictly controlled so the prices can be maintained in the domestic market.

5 The milk, egg and pork marketing boards are particularly aggressive advertisers. Advertising is also necessary to forestall declining demand. In 1989, the target price of industrial milk was increased and the quota volume reduced because demand was falling for dairy products in Canada.

6 J. C. Gilson, "World Agricultural Changes: Implications for Canada," (Toronto: C. D. Howe Institute, May, 1989), p. 64.

7 The real beneficiaries from this system are the original farmers who didn't have to pay for their quota. Anyone else who wants to be included might think twice about whether the entry fee is worth the price.

8 *The Financial Post*, 9 April 1990.

9 There is obvious concern that if agriculture is not supported, farmers will go bankrupt. In the early 1980s, thousands of farmers went out of business because of high interest rate payments. The problem in the early 1990s is due mainly to decreases in world commodity prices. Farm support systems, whether geared to manage supply, or pay farmers a certain level of world prices, are not designed to help indefinitely if prices fall over a long period of time.

10 Even banks see the writing on the wall and are discounting the value of farm quotas as collateral.

11 The Canada–U.S. Free Trade Agreement, signed in 1989, calls for complete free trade in cattle, hogs, and red meat sectors, but those products were trading practically under conditions of free trade to begin with. The removal of a few border irritants, such as tariffs and health regulations, should make it a little easier to move products between countries; and the elimination of tariffs should help Canadians sell more grains and canola oil in the United States. The agreement also calls for phasing out border restrictions and discrimination against the importation of American wine and liquor, although these restrictions were already being removed under the GATT.

MYTH 4

HIGHER MINIMUM WAGES ARE A GOOD WAY TO HELP THE WORKING POOR

Imagine trying to make ends meet in Toronto, or any major Canadian city, on a weekly salary of $216. At a wage of $5.40, that's what someone working at the minimum wage earns after a forty-hour week, or $864 a month before taxes and UI payments. After paying for rent and food, not even a financial wizard living on a diet of macaroni and cheese can scratch out a decent standard of living. It is hard enough for an individual, but compound the problem by adding a spouse and children. By anyone's definition, earning the minimum wage means poverty, pure and simple. In fact, Statistics Canada estimates that in 1988, in order to escape being classified as poor, a family of four had to earn at least $21,000, or twice the amount provided by the minimum wage, whether through work or social assistance.[1]

Some studies estimate that the working poor in Canada make up over 50 percent of the poor in our society. Thus, having a job is certainly no guarantee of escaping poverty although that's exactly what minimum wage legislation was designed to cure. It attempts to make sure that if people work, they will not be earning wages so low that they cannot provide the essentials of life.

As with many public policy programs, minimum wage legislation is designed to correct an "equity" problem in the system. Most of us would argue that it is only right that the working poor make a decent income — it is this equity principle that drives policy makers to distribute income from the haves to the have nots because we intrinsically believe that the poor are needier than the rich. That's why we have a progressive income tax system that requires those who earn more to pay a higher percentage of their income to taxes. But what about a policy that pretends to help the working poor by increasing their wages but in fact hurts the very group it was intended to help? By anyone's criteria, that would be totally unacceptable. Odd as it may seem, that's what minimum wage legislation actually does.

HOW DO MINIMUM WAGES HURT THE POOR?

To begin with, minimum wages are a form of price control for labour. In this case, there is a floor price under which wages can't fall. There is interference with what the cost of labour would normally have been without government intervention. The theory works something like this: If the forces of supply and demand in a free market economy determine that wages in a given sector are $5/hr. and the government dictates that they should be $6/hr., then there is a problem. At $6/hr. more people are willing to work, but fewer businesses are willing to hire. The result is an **excess** supply of labour or an increase in unemployment at the new wage rate (see Figure 4.1). What happens when employers are legislated by law to pay the higher minimum wage? Businesses have a number of choices: pay the higher labour costs; begin substituting capital or machinery for labour as the cost of labour goes up relative to capital; cut expenses by laying off some workers or cutting back on employee incentives; or in more drastic cases, shutdown operations and close up shop. Another alternative open to business is to pay workers illegally (under the table) in which case the taxpayer pays the higher costs of taxes forgone. In each situation, someone pays for the higher wage: either the worker by losing his job, or having his hours or incentives cut back; or the employer who absorbs the higher costs. In the more drastic case where the business closes down, everyone is worse off. This is the classic case of a zero sum gain where you can only better one group by making another worse off.

As with any government tampering with the price system, whether it involves commodities or wages, there are winners and losers. There is one type of winner — the ones who still have jobs at the higher wage. On the other hand, there are several types of losers. First is the employer who has to pay higher wages. One way or another the employer will try to get someone else to "foot the bill." Either they will pass the costs on (in which case the consumer loses out by paying higher prices), or they will have the employees themselves take on the burden of the higher labour costs. As already mentioned, the employer can decide not to hire an extra worker or can cut back the hours of those already employed. They can get their employees to work harder, thereby making the workers "earn their keep." Some employers have other ways of getting around the legislation, from hiring family members (who are often exempt from the legislation), to paying for labour in cash and thereby eluding detection and taxes altogether.

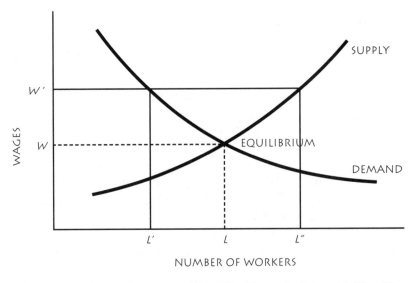

NOTE: In a free labour market, wages would be at W and the supply of labour at L. If the minimum wage by law goes to W', the supply of labour now goes to L''. The demand for labour drops to L', leaving an excess supply of workers, or a higher level of unemployment.

FIGURE 4.1   HOW MINIMUM WAGES LEAD TO INCREASED UNEMPLOYMENT

The second loser is the unemployed worker. If an employer makes the decision to let someone go or not to hire an extra worker in the future, the victim is likely to be a younger, less-experienced worker. This occurs in the stage of their careers during which they would usually be receiving training. Typically when workers enter the labour market their productivity is low and consequently they earn low wages. However, employers use this low-wage period to train their workers. This, in turn, allows workers to get a better foothold in the labour market. But if the minimum wage exceeds that paid to workers while they are being trained, employers tend to cut back on-the-job education. In the end society ends up with fewer trained workers and a reduction in human capital. The third and final victim, therefore, is the taxpayer because for those workers who can't find work because of the minimum wage law, the alternative is usually welfare and social assistance.

Not surprisingly, research confirms what theory tells us. Raising the minimum wage actually causes more unemployment, particularly among the young with the least job experience. An increase of 10 percent in the mimimum wage increases unemployment by about 1.4 percent for women and 1.5 percent for teenagers.[2] Once the young lose their jobs, there is little immediate prospect of finding more work. Therefore it should come as no surprise that the unemployment rate in the fifteen to twenty-four year old age group is always 5 percentage points higher than the rate for the entire labour force; and teenage unemployment is traditionally twice the national level. Yet despite the evidence that this anti-poverty theory does not work, the Left continues in their pursuit to "outlaw poverty."

POLICIES OF THE LEFT

When Ontario's New Democratic Party was elected in 1990, they made it clear they were going to boost the minimum wage from $5.40 per hour to 60 percent of the average industrial wage over the next five years. Based on an inflation rate of 2.5 percent over the intervening years, the minimum wage should average about $7.75 by 1995. But, as we have already seen, someone has to pay for the higher wage. In a study designed to measure the effects of Ontario's legislation, the Institute for Policy Analysis at the University of Toronto estimated that the NDP plan could cost the province almost 55,000 jobs.[3] Even a study commissioned by the Ontario Ministry of Labour estimated that a 10 percent increase in the minimum wage would cost about 25,000 jobs for Ontario.[4]

The group most affected by the NDP proposal is young, single women. According to the Ontario Ministry of Labour figures, of the 160,000 workers collecting the minimum wage (about 4.1 percent of the labour force), 57 percent of these are women, and only 22 percent are heads of households. So we see that in order to raise the wage of less than 5 percent of the labour force, the Ontario government is willing to jeopardize the jobs of thousands of workers. Is the cost worth the benefit?

What of the businesses that are required to pay the higher wages? It is important to keep in mind that it is not General Motors, Apple Inc., or Bell Canada that pays minimum wage; rather it is small businesses, the ones that have less leverage to begin with. Low wages are paid in the more marginalized and competitive sectors of the economy, such as fast-food restaurants, retail outlets, and a whole range of other low-skill operations. Only 9 percent of workers in manufacturing earn the minimum wage. The other 91 percent work in areas such as retail trade, and the hospitality industry. If these businesses are compelled to pay higher wages, *someone* has to pay for it. Poor wages can't be legislated out of existence without significant costs to both the worker, the employer, and society.

There are those who make the case that jobs lost to higher minimum wage legislation were not worth keeping anyway, that society is better off without them and that we can live without jobs like security guards, cleaning staff, and retail sales clerks. But these jobs are not completely without value. These are the jobs that allow the young to first enter the labour market and gain the experience and responsibility that they carry into adulthood. Many new immigrants rely on these jobs to get a foothold in the labour market, to allow them to acquire the skills to better their lot in society. Besides, if the intention of minimum wage laws are to ban or discourage certain types of jobs, it would be more effective to do so directly rather than as the side effect of laws that are supposed to improve the wages of working poor.[5]

If the public policy of imposing minimum wage legislation is so costly for society, why do governments bother? One answer is that it's simple and initially costless for governments. By simply legislating higher wages, it gives the impression that governments are doing something to help the working poor. It doesn't take much to pass legislation, even though it ends up creating enormous problems down the road. It's no different from the motivation that drives politicians to implement rent control. For governments, it's an expedient short-term solution to a long-run problem. Besides, it is politically harmless to trade off the benefits of the few known beneficiaries against the jobs of those yet to come into the labour market. The former group are a known quantity with political clout, while the latter workers, who bear the cost of the legislation, are not yet identified and will be looking for jobs sometime in the future.

It is not surprising that trade unions are the main supporters of minimum wage laws. Unions, essentially, want to present themselves as a labour cartel and have a united front when negotiating higher wages. It would not be in their best interest if nonunion workers were willing to perform identical services at lower wages. The higher the minimum wage, the greater the wage bargaining influence of labour. Another reason is that various occupations or trades maintain a constant wage difference between skill groups. For example, if electricians earn four times the minimum wage as a guide to wage negotiations, the higher the minimum wage, the higher the wages for electricians. Minimum wage legislation was a hard fought victory for labour that goes back to the 1930s, and they won't give it up without a fight.

WHAT IS TO BE DONE?

If legislating higher wages is not an effective way to help the working poor, what is? First of all, helping the working poor cannot be addressed simply as a wage problem — it's a social, educational and economic problem. As most low-wage earners are young, part of the solution lies in helping workers before they reach the labour market. That means keeping students in school as long as possible in order for them to get the skills they need for gainful employment. More than one-third of all high-school students never graduate, and the resultant low literacy rates are affecting Canada's ability to compete at home and abroad. Another solution is to revamp the entire apprenticeship program to help workers get the best on-the-job training possible. These problems aren't new; governments have known about them for years. Social programs such as unemployment insurance and welfare must not be a deterrent to work. Provincial and municipal governments have to cooperate to encourage welfare recipients to supplement their incomes by working part-time without endangering their welfare status. Minimum wage laws are not a remedy; only a palliative.

Another alternative is for Canada to move towards a guaranteed annual (or minimum) income. Our current system to eradicate poverty is a confusing assortment of social security and income support programs that inefficiently transfers income to the poor. Under these programs it costs society more than a dollar to get a dollar to the poor. It has been long advocated that one way around this dilemma is to provide the poor a secure minimum income that subsidizes them without costing them their jobs. The argument against a minimum income guarantee is that it will be a disincentive to work, but that doesn't seem to be the case according to a recent government study that found little evidence that people generally worked less when they received a minimum guaranteed income. (For more on this issue see Chapter 14.) If the results hold, the federal and provincial governments should seriously consider adopting a program nationwide and should get rid of the less-efficient, market-distorting programs such as minimum wage laws.

Despite the evidence that minimum wage laws only make the working poor worse off, politicians insist on using them to raise incomes. They seem to see the problem of low income in its most simple form. They think that by passing a law, the lot of the poor will automatically improve. Politicians have to learn the difference between the intent of the law and its actual effects. Minimum wage laws have exactly the opposite impact from those intended: more working poor and higher unemployment.

NOTES

[1] The irony should not escape anyone. The government sets a minimum wage and then turns around and says if you are not making twice that amount, you are classified as poor.

[2] Jean-Michel Cousineau, David Tessier and Francois Vaillancourt, *The Impact of the Ontario Minimum Wage on the Unemployment of Women and the Young: A Note*, Policy Study 91-6 (Toronto: Institute for Policy Analysis, University of Toronto, 1991), p. 5.

[3] Cousineau, Tessier and Vaillancourt, *The Impact of the Ontario Minimum Wage*.

[4] Peter Dungan and Morley Gunderson, *The Effect of Minimum Wage Increases on Employment in Ontario* (Toronto: Institute for Policy Analysis, University of Toronto, 1989).

[5] Another odd side effect of minimum wage laws is that they may be helping the wrong people. Although 30 percent of minimum wage earners had family earnings of $15,000 per year, 37 percent of those collecting minimum wages had total family earnings greater than $40,000. Minimum wages were going to part-time, teenage workers of wealthier families.

CANADA CAN'T COMPETE WITH INEXPENSIVE MEXICAN LABOUR

When Canadians think of Mexico, two images come to mind. There's the travel agent's version of sun, sand, colourful festivals, and rich Mayan and Spanish history. But when we think of commerce, Mexico becomes a nation of grinding poverty, oppressing population growth, with thousands of illegal aliens crossing the Rio Grande into the United States. Now Mexico becomes a nation of peasants toiling away for a few pesos a day, producing goods waiting to be exported and threatening our jobs and standard of living. The question arises, how can we compete with a nation that pays its labourers a fraction of the average Canadian wage? In other words, it seems to some that a rich country like Canada cannot trade with a poor one that has such an overwhelming competitive advantage. Ironically the same people who opposed the free trade agreement with the United States because they were worried that Canada couldn't compete with a bigger, richer nation are now opposed to free trade with Mexico because it is too poor.

Regardless of the theory and historical evidence to the contrary, this is one of the most enduring myths in international trade. The argument against Canada signing a North American Free Trade Agreement (NAFTA) is that without tariffs or nontariff barriers, industry and jobs would move where labour costs are lower. That's the perception but the reality is quite different. In order to dispel this myth, let's take a look at the theory and then the facts.

MORE TRADE IS BETTER THAN LESS

If there is one area of general agreement among economists, it's the benefits of free trade. The reasoning is that we should import any good that can be produced more cheaply abroad than if we tried to make it ourselves. Conversely, we should concentrate on those goods we can make at a lower cost than anyone else. This logic makes sense in both local commerce and international trade. For example, we don't think twice about buying bread from a bakery even though we could bake a better loaf ourselves. Yet no one argues that we should protect ourselves from the baker. Common sense tells us we should spend our time doing the things we do best.[1] In other words, we're better off if we specialize and then trade our goods and services.

That's why we buy shoes from Brazil, cameras from Japan, and coffee from Columbia. (Imagine the expense of growing our own coffee beans!) In turn we sell wood products, telecommunications equipment and wheat. We could try protecting our shoe producers with tariffs, but consumers would be worse off because they would pay higher prices without the quality and price they've come to expect. But what if, say, Korea could produce everything more efficiently than Canada? Wouldn't free trade make us worse off? The short answer is no.

To understand why, let's look at the example of a doctor who is a better typist than her secretary. Does this mean that she should fire her secretary and do her own paperwork? Of course not. Even if the doctor is a better typist, it would be more productive if the physician practised medicine and the secretary continued to type. Think of the inefficiency if the doctor tried to do both jobs. The same principle applies to nations.

Assume Canada has a large cost advantage over Mexico in the production of telecommunications equipment, but also has a small cost advantage in the assembly of electronic products. Canada would be better off specializing and putting its resources where it has a comparative advantage. The same goes for Mexico. In this case assume Canada specializes in telecommunications equipment, and Mexico assembles electronic products. In the end, both countries would have more of both goods.[2] In addition, as countries specialize, they also reap the benefits of lower production costs. This is known as economies of scale, which simply means the more that is produced, the lower the cost of each unit of production. In other words, we learn by doing.[3]

LOW PRODUCTIVITY MEANS LOW WAGES

Still, many people are not convinced by the above line of reasoning. Their biggest concern is the low level of Mexican wages. They argue either that jobs will be lost or wages will fall to the level of the lowest wage country or both. This is unlikely to happen.

There's no doubt that Mexican wages are low. The average unskilled Mexican worker makes $0.60 an hour (at the current exchange rate), while the Canadian wage for comparable labour is $6.00. (The average *industrial* wage is closer to $12.00 an hour in Canada.) But the cost of labour isn't the only factor that determines a nation's ability to compete. Just as important, if not more, is productivity — that is, how much can a Canadian worker produce over a given period of time compared to a Mexican worker? Here, Canadians are far ahead. Canadian workers on the whole are more productive than those in Mexico because they have a lot more machinery and capital to work with. They're also better educated and have more skills. Labour is paid according to how productive it is. That's why Canadians earn higher wages.[4]

Mexican firms on the other hand fear high productivity levels in Canada. But there is an awareness that lower productivity, not free trade, brings lower wages and that lower standards of living follow. In the past, protectionism has been used to solve the problem but has failed. Mexico can benefit if it specializes in those goods that take advantage of its low wages, while Canada can concentrate on goods that require more capital. Mexico realizes that protectionism and inward-looking policies that isolated its industries from competition over the last half-century are to blame for its poverty, and not free trade. That's why it wants a free trade deal with the United States and Canada.

As to the argument that Canadian wages would fall to Mexican levels, that would happen only if both countries produced one and the same product and workers were equally productive. Both countries produce thousands of different products that range over hundreds of industries, all requiring different levels of skills and training.

Those who remain unconvinced about the removal of tariffs on Mexican products should consider the following: the average tariff imposed by Canada on goods coming in from Mexico is only 10 percent. The tariff turns the cost of $0.60 an hour in the domestic market into $0.66 an hour for the export market. That hardly gives the Canadian worker much of an advantage. If we really wanted relief from Mexican wages, tariffs would have to be at least 100 percent! If we can't compete with Mexico when wages are $0.60 an hour, but can at $0.66, then there must be something wrong with the low-wage argument.[5]

Then there's the myth that jobs will automatically move to Mexico if tariffs are lowered. Given that Mexican wages are low and that existing tariffs aren't high enough to protect domestic workers, the obvious question is why haven't jobs left before this? The reason is that the cost of labour is only one factor in many that determine where industry locates. Companies also have to consider factors such as transportation facilities, communications services, and the supply of skilled and reliable labour.

TRADE HAS MADE CANADA PROSPEROUS

Critics of free trade with Mexico argue that these ideas may work in theory, but have no place in the real world. The evidence suggests otherwise. Since Canada became a member of the General Agreement on Tariffs and Trade (GATT) in 1947, it has reduced its trade barriers not only against high-wage, but also against low-wage countries. Since the 1930s, Canada has reduced its trade barriers against all countries by 80 percent. Whole industries haven't disappeared, but the nature of the work has changed. We have moved toward higher-paying, more productive jobs, and away from low-paying, low value-added ones.[6] This was achieved with more trade, not less. One-third of everything we consume is imported, and the same share of everything we make is exported. In other words, Canada has an open economy that relies heavily on the international market for its standard of living. Without trade we would have a radically different economy and a poorer one at that.[7]

Even when a country decides to use tariffs to protect a given sector of the economy from foreign competition, in effect it is redistributing income from one sector of the economy to another. Traditionally, for example, Canada used tariffs and quotas to protect the shoe industry from imports from low-cost producers in the Far East and Brazil. These tariffs turned out to be an expensive way of protecting jobs and distributing income.[8] It makes more sense to move the worker out of the shoe industry and retain him or her at government expense.

If we know how inefficient trade barriers are, why don't we get rid of them? The answer, as is so often the case, is that these policies are allowed to continue because a well-defined vested-interest group brings political pressure to bear, while thousands of consumers who pay a few dollars more for protected products are ignored.[9] As with any measure to protect an industry from competition, the interests of one group are traded away for the interests of another. Those who benefit from protection have an interest in maintaining the barriers. Tariffs and quotas protect high-cost, inefficient producers at the expense of the consumers who pay higher costs. At that point protected firms no longer have the incentives to become more efficient producers.

THERE WILL BE ADJUSTMENTS

As with any form of exchange, there will be costs along with the benefits. That is the essence of international trade. Without it, there would be no need to trade. Currently there is surprisingly little trade

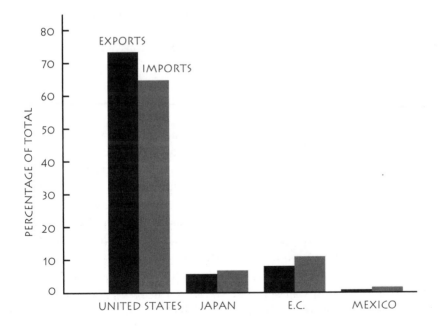

Source: StatsCan.

FIGURE 5.1 CANADA'S PERCENTAGE OF TRADE WITH SELECTED COUNTRIES 1990

between Canada and Mexico. In 1990, only 0.5 percent of all Canadian exports went to Mexico, while Mexican exports made up 1 percent of all our imports. Freer trade between the two countries suggests that there will be plenty of scope from the benefits of specialization and trade.

Our experience with Japan shows what can happen when markets remain open to trade expansion rather than trade restriction. Japan first started making tremendous inroads into our market in the 1970s and today we no longer compete with them on goods such as TVs, sound equipment, and cameras. Consumers can now buy high-quality products at prices lower than we could have ever produced them at ourselves. Has our economy suffered in the process? Even with Japan's vast penetration of our markets over the last twenty years, the Canadian economy was still able to create over 4.5 million jobs. In other words, we did adjust. Canadians shouldn't worry about a more prosperous Mexico, we should welcome it. As Mexico increases its standard of living, it becomes a larger market for Canadian exports.

Freer trade with Mexico means that Canada will lose jobs in the low-wage, more labour-intensive sectors. But we will gain more employment in the higher-wage export sectors. It has been estimated that Canada will lose between 5,000 to 6,000 jobs with freer trade with Mexico, but approximately 12,000 new jobs will be created. The winners will be concentrated in banks, construction firms, Ontario auto assembly plants and Prairie grain farms. The main job losses will be in auto parts manufacturing. Overall Canadian–Mexican trade will grow about 30 percent by 1995.[10] In the end, Canada will have access to another 85 million consumers. Given that there will be adjustments to trade, the government shouldn't ignore those most affected by more open markets. It has to commit resources to help workers adjust with more education and training programs (something the federal government failed to do after the free trade agreement was signed with the United States).

The adage that "no country was ever destroyed by trade" is true for Canada. Indeed, Canada's prosperity can be attributed to its ability to compete internationally. Countries that try to remain self-sufficient are the ones that suffer the most. Until recently, one of the most isolated countries in terms of trade was Albania. It's also one of the world's poorest. In today's economic environment, where prosperity comes from the ability to compete at home and abroad, any policy that simply protects jobs is self-defeating. If we ever want to see poorer countries prosper, the best way is to open our markets to their products rather than supplying them with hand-outs and charity. In the end, both rich and poor countries will be better off.

NOTES

1 Few in Canada would argue that Ontario should protect itself from lower wages in Newfoundland. However this does happen. Until recently, Canadian beer prices were higher than they needed to be because of inter-provincial trade restrictions.

2 Canada has a comparative advantage in telecommunications because it is more efficient and has lower costs than Mexico. The same applies to Mexico in auto parts production. Both countries can have more of both if they specialize and trade. This powerful, but not always obvious, truth was developed by the great nineteenth century economist David Ricardo who showed that a rich country could profitably trade with a low-wage country.

3 Economists estimate that the main benefits from the Canada–U.S. Free Trade Agreement would be generated from *economies of scale*. Producers would benefit because their input costs would be lower as suppliers passed on their savings up the production chain.

4 In economic theory, labour is paid according to its *marginal product*. The more it brings to total production, the higher the wage or *returns to that factor of production*. The same principle applies to other factors of production such as land or capital.

5 Richard Lipsey, "Canada at the U.S.–Mexico Free Trade Dance: Wallflower or Partner?", *Commentary* (Toronto: C.D. Howe Institute, August 1990.) Professor Lipsey is an eloquent exponent of freer trade with Mexico.

6 The European Community discarded the argument that it could not trade and compete with low-wage countries such as Portugal, Spain, and Greece when these countries were given full membership into the EC.

7 Since the late 1960s, Canada has had a balance of trade surplus with the rest of the world with the exception of three years in the mid 1970s when oil prices drove the account into deficit. Otherwise, Canada exports more goods and services than it imports.

8 To give an example of how costly and counterproductive tariffs can become, before quotas were removed in the shoe industry, it cost consumers $100,000 for every job protected in the footwear sector. It would have been cheaper for the taxpayer to pay the shoe worker not to work and import the shoes without protection. The same logic can be applied to other goods protected by import barriers. Under the guise of protecting jobs, they in fact sustain inefficiency and higher costs.

9 A more subtle cost of removing trade barriers entails trading jobs today for potentially better jobs tomorrow. It's hard to give up a sure thing now for the promise of more benefits in the future. That's why so many find the concept of free trade difficult to accept.

10 *The Globe and Mail* (28 February 1992), p. B4.

MYTH 6
CANADIAN MANUFACTURING IS DISAPPEARING

There is a common anxiety among Canadians that our economy has feet of clay. The argument goes something like this: the structure of the Canadian economy is built on an unstable service sector with too many government jobs, retail outlets, banks, fast-food operations, and foreign-owned companies that are glorified warehouses for goods produced outside the country. The idea is that we have become rich simply by "taking in each other's laundry." In other words, we really don't produce anything, we just move things around. Furthermore, the argument goes, the whole operation does nicely when the North American economy is booming, but during a recession this tenuous structure will come crashing down like a house of cards.

Although most of us work in the service industry, and the majority of jobs are in that sector, we somehow feel that they are less valuable than the "real" jobs found in manufacturing and resources. We believe that an economy's wealth is based on output in the goods-producing sector, and feel that the country could use more manufacturing jobs in autos, aerospace, and computers; and know that we could certainly get along with fewer lawyers, civil servants, and personal services. This general unease about services is aggravated by the sense that Canada's economy is suffering from deindustrialization, and that the "real" jobs are moving south of the border or off-shore altogether.

Is that the reality? Is Canada moving from a nation once based on resources and manufacturing to one of fast-food outlets and video arcades? The simple answer is no. This myth has two misconceptions: first, that the more valuable manufacturing jobs are being lost at an alarming rate; and second, that the service jobs replacing them are inferior and less useful to society. The truth is, manufacturing isn't dead in Canada, and our economy is not being hollowed out and replaced with second-rate jobs.[1] What *has* changed is the nature of manufacturing. Along with that, there has been a greater blurring between goods and services.

MANUFACTURING STILL MATTERS

The transition from a goods-producing economy to a service-oriented one is similar to the switch from an agricultural to an industrial economy at the turn of the century. At that time there was concern that as people moved from farms to the city there would not be enough farmers left to feed the urban society. But North America became an industrial economy largely because of the rapid productivity growth in agriculture. The same type of transformation is taking place today, as we move from goods to services because of the rapid productivity growth in goods production.[2] This growth in manufacturing over the last thirty years has allowed employment to shift from the factory to services: a natural transition in the development of any advanced industrial country.[3] However, just as the eighteenth-century group know as the Physiocrats believed that real wealth came only from the land and not from factories, modern-day beliefs hold that services are less valuable than goods.

The first question to ask is, has manufacturing or the production of goods dropped off as a share of gross domestic product? It may surprise some to know that it hasn't. Over the last thirty years, manufacturing continued to account for about 50 percent of all goods production, which includes agriculture, natural resources and manufactured products. Manufacturing still makes up about 20 percent of GDP and has remained at that level for decades (see Figure 6.1). What has changed is the number of jobs in manufacturing. In 1960, manufacturing employed over 30 percent of the labour force; by 1989, that figure dropped to under 16 percent. Even with the drop in the share of manufacturing jobs throughout the 1980s, the absolute number of jobs increased from 1.6 million in 1984 to 1.9 million in 1989. From 1982 to 1989, jobs in the goods-producing sector increased 1.5 percent on an average annual basis, but service jobs went up 2.7 percent. The drop in relative employment was not the result of manufacturing becoming less important to the economy. The decline in the manufacturing share of Canada's total number of jobs indicates the greater use of technology in the manufac-

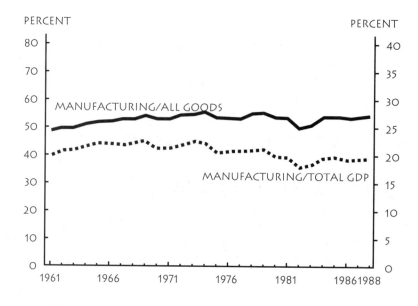

PERCENT   PERCENT

MANUFACTURING/ALL GOODS

MANUFACTURING/TOTAL GDP

1961   1966   1971   1976   1981   19861988

NOTE: Left scale represents manufacturing as a percentage of all goods produced. Right scale represents manufacturing as a share of total GDP in the economy.

Source: StatsCan.

FIGURE 6.1   THE IMPORTANCE OF MANUFACTURING TO THE ECONOMY

turing process and higher productivity. Canadian industry is producing the same level of output with fewer workers. One of the reasons is that virtually all research and development spending is in manufacturing or goods production. In 1987, R&D spending in manufacturing averaged $1,500 compared with only $150 in services.

If anything has changed it is how the number of manufacturing jobs is expanding and contracting more rapidly in response to economic swings. Employers are reacting to economic changes more quickly by hiring and releasing workers faster than they have in the past. In recessions before 1980, there was an average five-month lag between cuts in output and cuts in employment. That is no longer the case. For the recessions of 1981 and 1990, the production and employment cuts were virtually simultaneous. The high cost of labour and competitive pressures to increase productivity are forcing companies to respond much more quickly to downturns in the economy. They no longer have the luxury of holding onto workers as they wait for the economy to improve. This gives the impression that manufacturing jobs are more at risk now than in the past, and that once they're gone, they're gone for good. But this is not so. A more accurate description would be that when manufacturing changes, the jobs associated are changed forever. That does not mean that manufacturing is dead. It does signify that the pace of manufacturing change is quicker and with it the way we employ labour.

THE NEW ROLE OF SERVICES

Even the increase in services has to be understood in the context of a changing economy. Services do not exist in a vacuum. As the needs of the economy change, so does the service sector. Also, the gap between the goods-producing and service sectors are often exaggerated. Many services use tangible goods such as computers; and many goods-producing businesses contract substantial service-oriented businesses (such as outside lawyers and accountants) to do work that was once provided by professionals on their own staffs. Manufacturers still need these services, but they no longer retain the people who provide them on permanent staff. It is less expensive to contract the work from outside. Since the 1981–82 recession, firms are coming under greater pressure to increase their level of specialization and are contracting out more of their work to the service sector.

But not all service jobs are created equally. There is a world of difference between a short-order cook and a highly trained nurse. Not surprisingly, it was high-powered service jobs (e.g., accounting, marketing, and legal) that helped propel the Canadian economy during the latter part of the last decade. These dynamic, high-paying jobs in business, along with those in health, education and public administration, accounted for 60 percent of the increase in service sector jobs in Canada from 1983 to 1988, compared to 29 percent in the lower-paying traditional services, such as personal services, retail, and food services.[4]

Within these services, the fastest growing ones are related directly to business, such as computers, management consulting, and advertising. In 1986, the service industries provided more than half of the jobs classified as "high-tech." Within this high-tech sector, 55 percent were in services to business management, and 45 percent in the finance industries. These jobs are growing *because of* manufacturing, not in spite of it. A dynamic service sector is essential for maintaining the competitiveness and health of the nation's manufacturing base. It seems irrelevant to ask which is more important, a manufacturing job making a specific product, or the truck-driving service taking it to market. In the final analysis, both are just as important in getting the product into the hands of the consumer.

As manufacturing and services become more interrelated, the lines between them are becoming more clouded. For instance, one might ask, does Xerox provide goods or services? In many ways manufacturing firms are behaving more like services. Walking through an automated car plant, the level of information technology is such that services are becoming an ever bigger part of the production process. The growing need for better and faster information on the part of the service industry drives the need for better equipment and hardware, which in turn drives the need for better information. Gone are the days when services and goods were distinct commodities bearing little relationship to each other.[5]

A common criticism of services has been the lower level of productivity, as measured by output per employee, compared to manufacturing. The obvious implication is that we should have more manufacturing if we want to improve our standard of living. Productivity in goods production from 1964 to 1984 has grown twice as fast as that of services. The average increase per annum was 4.6 percent, compared to 2.2 percent for services. Part of the growth in goods production was the impressive growth in agriculture productivity; but even if we eliminate that, we still get a growth rate of 3.9 percent for goods. However, since 1973 that gap has been narrowing. Not all services have been slow in productivity improvement. Productivity in transportation, utilities and the communications sector grew at almost twice the rate of the manufacturing sector. Some analysts have also argued that service productivity is a statistical illusion and current forms of measurement underestimate the growth of service productivity.[6]

Compounding the problem of measurement is the issue of quality improvements in the service sector. It's relatively easy to measure output in dollars and cents when it comes to goods; it's a different story when quality is being assessed. How do you measure the quality of a day in hospital, the convenience of 24-hour banking, or the satisfaction derived from a Broadway play? The problem is even worse in nonmarket services where there isn't even the benefit of an objective market price. How do you measure the value of a good teacher, social worker, the Cancer Foundation, defence, police protection, and other services that are provided free or at a small fraction of their true costs? Although there's an attempt to measure quality improvements in marketed services, no systematic records are kept for the nonmarketed ones.

Despite the integration and rising importance of services in the economy, there is one role that goods production plays that is not matched by services: goods still dominate in international trade and allow Canada to maintain a positive trade balance. Ninety-nine percent of manufactured goods, and 97 percent of the primary sector (i.e. agriculture and natural resources) compete at home and in the international market, compared with only 3 percent of all business services. Services as a share of total exports is only 12.5 percent, the lowest for all the Organization for Economic Co-operation and Development (OECD) nations.[7] The services we do trade are tourism, consulting engineering, and financial services. The sectors that have no international component are education, personal services, utilities and government. In 1987, Canada exported about $126 billion in merchandise trade and only $18 billion in services. Canada usually maintains a balance of trade surplus in goods production, but we traditionally run a trade deficit in services, mainly because we travel abroad so much. In time that will change as the techniques for how we measure trade in services improves. Better measurement of trade in services may very well reduce our trade deficit in services. Again, services and goods production we send abroad depend upon each other. An efficient domestic service sector makes our products more competitive internationally.

NOTES

[1] The U.S. economy is experiencing a comeback in its "rust belt" states. In a study by the Department of Commerce, it was found that manufacturing has staged a revival over the past ten years. It seems that fears of deindustrialization were exaggerated. U.S. manufacturing as a percentage of GNP climbed from 21 percent in 1960 to 23 percent in 1990.

[2] At the turn of the century, almost 40 percent of the labour force were in agriculture. Today only 3 percent work in farming and primary industry. A similar change-over has happened from the goods-producing sector to services. Around 1958 there was an equal share of jobs in services and goods production. Today almost 70 percent of the jobs are in services and 30 percent in goods.

3 From 1966 to 1986, Canada saw a decline of 6.7 percent in the share of workers in manufacturing, while Germany's share fell 9.1 percent, the United States by 10 percent and Japan by 5.7 percent. Source: OECD and Statistics Canada.

4 The Economic Council of Canada, *Goods Jobs, Bad Jobs, Employment in the Service Economy* (Ottawa: Supply and Services, 1990).

5 The great economist Alfred Marshall felt that there is little distinction between goods and services in the sense that man simply readjusts matter in order to "create" a good. In this sense, all commercial activity is a service of one kind or another, and one shouldn't exaggerate the distinction between goods and services.

6 "The Growth of Services in the Canadian Economy," Statistics Canada, *Canadian Economic Observer*, January 1988, p. 33.

7 Economic Council of Canada, *Employment in the Service Economy* (Ottawa: Supply and Services, 1991), p. 16.

MYTH 7

CANADIANS CAN'T COMPETE

The perception that Canadians are no longer competitive is quickly becoming a truism. Hardly a day passes without an article or news item lamenting our declining productivity, poor R & D record, a growing trade deficit in high-tech products, an ill-trained labour force, and overall inability to compete with our major trading partners. One newspaper editorial went on at length about the fact that on a worldwide basis, Canada slipped from fourth to fifth place among a total of twenty-four developed countries in our overall ability to compete in 1990. The article argued that we were on the long slippery slide to decline.[1] The implication was that unless we "pull up our socks" and do something about our faltering ability to compete, we'll fall victim to the British disease, lose our international markets and become a third world country. If we say it enough times, any data that might suggest otherwise becomes suspect and untrustworthy.

ALL THE NEWS SEEMS BAD

A small industry has been spawned looking for competitive weaknesses in the Canadian economy, and sure enough they end up finding them even when the data is questionable. One example is a study commissioned by Kodak.[2] The study starts with a summary of Canada's ability to compete based on the World Competitiveness Report prepared annually by a group of European academics.[3] The report summarizes a country's ability to compete based on ten criteria ranging from industrial efficiency to human resources and sociopolitical stability. In some areas Canada ranks high (e.g., natural resource endowment) and in others we perform badly (e.g., international orientation). In other words, our presence in other markets via exports does not have much of a profile. As interesting as this ranking is, it isn't very scientific. Rankings are based on impressions and perceptions of executives from around the world. As with most impressions and perceptions, they change as easily as opinions. A case in point is Italy. In 1990 it ranked eighteenth in a slate of twenty-four countries. On the business confidence scale, it was just ahead of Hungary. Germany and Japan ranked number one and two. On this basis one would expect Italy to perform dismally on the international markets but the truth is quite the opposite. Based on the same report, Italy had one of the world's fastest growing export markets, ranking just behind Japan. Throughout the 1980s Italy had one of the fastest growing economies in Europe and an extremely productive manufacturing sector.[4] Why, then, was there an oversight? Most of the experts looked at Italy's political and social situations, its massive national debt and wrote the country off without getting behind the perceptions. The rise of Italy's small manufacturing industries has been one of the greatest success stories in Europe over the past decade.

The Kodak study also claimed that Canada had a lower than average level of manufacturing productivity growth rate from 1981 to 1987 at 3.8 percent. Was that a poor performance? Compared to Japan, with a productivity growth rate of 6.2 percent, the answer is yes. Germany, one of the world's economic powerhouses, had to settle for a disappointing 2 percent. The real surprise was Britain, with an average manufacturing productivity growth rate of 5.4 percent.

If someone had instead picked up a copy of the OECD Economic Outlook report for 1990, instead of the Kodak report, the results would have looked much different. From 1979 to 1988, the U.S. total labour productivity growth rate (output per employed person) averaged a mere 0.8 percent compared to Canada's 1.4 percent.[5] The Ontario government premier's report entitled Competing in the Global Economy was also a litany of complaints and bad news about Canada's capacity to make it in the rough-and-tumble world of international trade. That report lined up an impressive list of evidence to show how badly we are doing in training, R & D, patent registrations, number of engineers and scientists compared to Japan and the small number of technology intensive industries in Canada with positive trade balances. The picture was not a pretty one. The Ontario study concluded that Ontario is losing the battle to remain competitive and that "the opportunities and decisions we now face will determine the level of prosperity available to the next generation."[6] But the report found bad news even where none exists. It claimed that Canada's high growth, high value-added industries, such as the telecommunications industry, "is tremendously uncompetitive."[7] That would come as news to Northern Telecom, one of the world's most successful telecommunications companies. The study went on to show how we are losing ground to the Japanese, but we seem to be gaining on the Americans. When about 75 percent of all our trade is with the United States, that is the market we should be competitive with.

Academic studies and government reports are not exempt from faulty analysis and erroneous conclusions. The Canadian Manufacturers Association in a report entitled The Aggressive Economy[8] rehashes the same tired data about R & D, patents and lack of a coherent government strategy. One of their major claims is that Canadian companies do not get enough tax incentives to carry out the necessary research and development when compared to other countries. Yet by their own admission Canada has the most generous incentives for R & D of all the G7 countries. This was backed up by a study conducted by the Conference Board of Canada, which concluded that "Canada's tax treatment of R & D conducted by large manufacturing companies remains the most favourable among the ten major industrial countries examined."[9]

There is nothing new about these studies; they have been around for years telling the government, business and whoever else would listen that our economy is declining and that we are becoming less competitive. In 1985 the Institute for Research on Public Policy came out with a report that forewarned of grave things because the Japanese overtook us in real output per hour in total manufacturing in 1979. The study cautioned that "if we continue, Canadian products will become uncompetitive in world markets. Exports will be threatened, and lower priced imports will replace domestic products in the Canadian domestic market."[10] This same report forecast that unemployment in the 1980s would remain high because industry, in order to remain cost competitive, would produce more with less labour; and a sure sign that things are deteriorating is the increase in structural unemployment caused by rapid changes in the economy. The study saw persistently high unemployment rates, and permanent job losses in secondary and primary sectors. By the end of the decade the study was wrong on both counts. Unemployment rates were down to single digits and we had the second highest employment growth rates among G7 countries after the United States. From 1983 to 1990, Canada produced almost two million new jobs and the unemployment rate fell from 11.8 percent to 8.1 percent before the 1990 recession. No G7 country has come close to matching Canada's ability to create jobs over the last three decades.

ANOTHER LOOK AT THE DATA

Many of these studies define competitiveness as the ability to sell products on the international market and achieve an increase in the balance of trade. A lack of exports may be due to poor monetary policy rather than a fundamental loss in competitiveness. The Bank of Canada's high interest rate, strong dollar policy made it hard for domestic exporters, while at the same time made foreign goods relatively cheaper in Canada.[11] One Canadian study estimated that with a less stringent monetary policy (i.e., lower interest rates) by 1991 Canada would have had a real trade balance improvement of $10 billion. It is true that wages have increased more in Canada than with our major trading partners, averaging 5.7 percent over the past decade. Now there are real signs that those rates are coming down, bringing wage increases in line with those in the United States.

But there are other ways to look at competitiveness rather than tallying up what we export or import. One way is to measure improvements in our standard of living. On this score, how does Canada's performance compare to the rest of the world? It may surprise many, but here is where we come into our own. In terms of living standard, Canada is a very rich country indeed and the envy of the world.

Although Canada trailed most G7 countries in the rate of productivity growth, the above studies fail to tell us Canada's absolute level of productivity compared to other countries. Despite our lagging productivity performance, from 1970 to 1990 Canada maintained the second highest level of GDP per employee after the United States. Canada is a high productivity, high income country, but the Japanese and Europeans have gained ground over the past two decades. Nonetheless these gains have to be put into perspective. The income and productivity gap narrowed as Japan and Europe rebuilt their economies after the war. The Japanese and European productivity rates were impressive after the Second World War because they were able to rebuild their factories with the latest technology. Japan and Europe also did not experience a population explosion brought on by a baby boom. That meant they invested in more labour-saving, and consequently more productive, capital equipment. In time productivity rates began to converge as countries adopted the best available technology. Even the Japanese rates are showing signs of slowing as their overall levels of productivity reach North American levels. Although other countries are catching up, Canada still maintains a remarkably impressive record.

Another standard of living indicator is how much GDP there is for each Canadian. For 1990 Canada ranked second behind the United States at 95 percent of the American level.[12] On this basis Germany is at 76 percent of the U.S. level and Japan at 80 percent.

Much has been said about our poor growth performance in terms of GDP; but how does Canada stack up with other G7 countries? Over the past thirty years the average G7 country's economy grew by a rate of 3.8 percent while Canada's grew by 4.2 percent per annum. This is not bad for a country that is supposed to be losing its competitive edge (see Figure 7.1). Another indicator, compiled by the United Nations, is known as the Human Development Index. This measures three key components: national income, literacy and longevity. For 1991 Canada ranked first of all OECD countries. That was an improvement from sixth place in 1985. In other

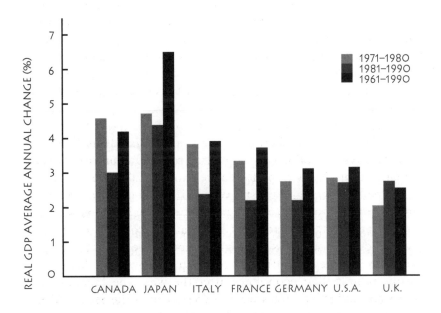

Source: StatsCan.

FIGURE 7.1   CHANGES IN GDP BY COUNTRY

words, Canada was the envy of the world in terms of a place to live and work. As far as work is concerned, Canada has one of the best-trained and educated labour forces in the world, and that in itself is perhaps the most important asset any country can have when it comes to competing and maintaining a high standard of living. One final test is that foreign investors are still putting their money into Canada. By the late 1980s Canada was undergoing its biggest foreign investment boom. We had $10 billion more invested in Canada than we invested abroad.

SERIOUS PROBLEMS REMAIN

This is not to suggest that Canada does not have any problems or that we should downplay the real ones that exist. The point is that data comparing intercountry performance can be confusing and often missing altogether, depending on different data collection techniques, base years, and average annual percentage changes over various periods. The main problem with most of these studies is that good, consistent information is hard to get. By the time data is published, the thing one is trying to measure has most likely changed. Competitiveness is a complex creature that is constantly undergoing change. Some industries or countries have unlocked the mysteries of the puzzle while others struggle to keep up.

Canada does face difficult competitive challenges, and will face more in the future. Competing in international markets is not easy, nor will it be in the future. Many of the above studies and reports do make the valid observation that the nature of competition between nations is undergoing radical change and that what made us rich in the past cannot be assumed to be able to make us well-off in the future. That is the main message of the study undertaken by Michael Porter of the Harvard Business School.[13] In a study commissioned by the federal government and Business Council on National Issues, Professor Porter argues that Canada can't rely on its resource base to maintain its standard of living. In the world of the future, wealth will be created and not inherited.

Canada has undergone drastic structural changes in the past twenty to thirty years and in the process has provided a standard of living for its citizens that has been envied by the rest of the world. However, the country is not standing still. NAFTA trade talks, deregulation, tax reform and knocking down internal provincial trade barriers will go a long way in helping Canada meet growing international competition. But we are changing. Today, communications and telecommunications employ more people than mining and petroleum combined.

Everyone agrees that productivity should be improved, but the problem for the governments of Canada is that many of these reports prescribe different solutions to the problem of growing international competition. Where the private sector through the Canadian Manufacturing Association calls for more deregulation of industry, Michael Porter argues that more stringent and selective regulation may actually be beneficial in forcing some industries to become more competitive. Should more money go to more apprenticeship programs or R & D supported government projects? These questions will always be a challenge to policy makers. Allocating scarce resources has always been a problem, but that is not a sign of competitive weakness. There is no guarantee that we will prosper, or be as successful in the coming years, but minimizing our achievements is not the solution.

NOTES

[1] The Financial Post (June 1990), editorial page.

[2] Alan Rugman and Joseph D'Cruz, Fast Forward: Improving Canada's International Competitiveness (Toronto: Faculty of Management, University of Toronto, 1989), p. 8.

[3] The report defines competitiveness as "the ability of entrepreneurs to design, produce and market goods and services, the price and non-price characteristics of which form a more attractive package than that of competitors." See The World Competitiveness Report 1989 (Geneva: IMEDE and World Economic Forum, 1989).

[4] U.S. Bureau of Labour Statistics, International Comparisons of Manufacturing Productivity and Labour Costs Trends, 1988, June 1989.

By 1990, Italy had the fourth highest GDP per employee levels in the world (adjusted by purchasing-power parities), behind Canada, which was third. See Government of Canada, Canadian Federalism and Economic Union: Partnership for Prosperity, (Ottawa: Supply and Services, 1991).

[5] OECD, Economic Outlook, December 1990.

[6] Report of the Premier's Council, Competing in the New Global Economy (Toronto: Queen's Printer for Ontario, 1989).

[7] Competing in the New Global Economy

8   The Aggressive Economy: Daring to Compete (Toronto: Canadian Manufacturer's Association, June 1989).

9   Jacek Warda, International Competitiveness of Canadian R&D Tax Incentives: An Update (Ottawa: Conference Board of Canada, May 1990).

10 Joseph D'Cruz and James Fleck, Canada Can Compete! Strategic Management of the Canadian Industrial Portfolio (Montreal: Institute for Research on Public Policy, 1985).

11 That was the conclusion of WEFA Canada, an economic consulting group. They also showed that with a less-stringent monetary policy, Canada's manufacturing employment would have shed 100,000 fewer jobs in manufacturing, and the nation would have had $60 billion less in debt. See Why Has Canada's Economy Performed So Badly? (WEFA, March 1992) pp. 43–44.

12 Canada's per capita real GDP was adjusted for purchasing-power parity (PPP), which is designed to correct for distortions in the market exchange rate. The PPP is defined by the OECD as "the rates of currency conversion that equalize the purchasing power of different currencies." This is a way of comparing the countries' currencies and purchasing power. For example, a given sum of money, when converted into different currencies at the PPP rate, will buy the same basket of goods and services in all countries.

13 Michael E. Porter, Canada at the Crossroads: The Reality of a New Competitive Environment (prepared for the Business Council on National Issues and the Government of Canada, 1991).

MYTH 8

THE FTA WAS A BAD DEAL FOR CANADA

F
ew policies or programs caused as much divisiveness in the country as the Free Trade Agreement (FTA) signed with the United States and put into effect January 1, 1989. Canadians have been arguing about whether or not we got a good deal ever since. Those who opposed the deal, such as labour groups, Canadian nationalists, political scientists in general and the NDP, still claim that Canada got a bad deal. Other groups, made up of big business, Conservatives and academic economists feel that Canada was right to go ahead with the agreement. Both sides can provide numbers defending their arguments. Free trade opponents claim that Canada has lost over 350,000 jobs to free trade and that manufacturing jobs are going south where the cost of production is less expensive. Those who supported the deal argue that the purpose of the agreement was to increase trade between the two countries, creating more jobs in the long run.

Again the average citizen has been left in the dark about whether Canada made the right decision. The truth of the matter is that it is too early to tell; however, the more credible data tends to suggest that so far the gains are positive but small. It only stands to reason that if there were not gains to be made on both sides, an agreement would never have been signed. That is the essence of international trade. But how much we have gained is a question we will have to wait years to assess fully.[1]

If that's the case, why do so many people feel we have been "had" by the Americans and the Mulroney government? Part of the answer lies in politics rather than economics and in what people saw the agreement to be in the first place. Another part is that the FTA came into effect just before the country entered the 1990 recession and it was inevitable that opponents of the agreement would confuse the hardships of the recession with the signing of the free trade agreement. The Bank of Canada's high interest rate policy in

1990 and 1991 did not make matters any easier. Tight monetary policy had the desired effect of dampening demand and bringing down inflation, but at the cost of lost jobs.[2] To understand the agreement, and whether Canada got a good deal, it's important to understand the main reasons why Canada wanted the deal in the first place; then one can judge better whether the effort and years of negotiations were worth it.

WHY THE GOVERNMENT WANTED THE FTA

The Mulroney government wanted an agreement for three main reasons: first, to remove tariffs and reduce the cost of production for domestic manufacturing industry; second, to secure access to the U.S. market for Canadian goods; and third, as the basis for a new industrial policy to bring about restructuring and adjustment in the Canadian economy. Let's look at each in turn and assess whether Canada got what it wanted.

The first argument or justification for free trade is mainly an economic one. In order to overcome Canada's disadvantage as a high-cost producer, economists have often complained that Canada's small domestic market made it difficult to achieve what they call economies of scale. One way countries can reduce production costs is by concentrating on production in which they have a comparative advantage, or where they have lower opportunity costs (see Myth 5). Countries should allocate their resources in the production of goods or services where they have a comparative advantage and then trade among themselves for the products they do not produce. This way everyone will be better off. That is the simplified theory behind freer trade and the main reason economists support unfettered movement of goods and resources between countries without interference from tariffs or nontariff barriers.

But what is simple in theory, is harder in reality. Specialization and free trade mean that what a country produces tomorrow may not be what it produces today. It is understandable why some labour groups, especially in those sectors of the economy that face stiff international competition, would oppose freer trade.

Free trade with the United States would give Canadian producers greater access to a market ten times as large and reduce costs to domestic producers by not forcing them to pay tariffs for goods they import. In time Canadian firms would learn to adapt.

MYTH 8 — THE FTA WAS A BAD DEAL FOR CANADA

Although this may sound like a risky venture, there was evidence that Canadian producers could "take the heat." A number of economic studies showed that if tariffs were removed, domestic production would increase, and so would jobs and our standard of living.[3] That was the same logic that led the Royal Commission chaired by Donald Macdonald in 1985 to recommend that Canada pursue a free trade agreement with the United States. Macdonald said it would be a "leap of faith," but the risks were worth the potential gains in jobs and output.

Few disagreed that tariffs should be removed. In fact, over 80 percent of the goods flowing between the United States and Canada were crossing the border duty free. The FTA would get rid of the remaining 20 percent over a ten year period. Granted, the remaining higher tariffs were on manufactured goods, such as textiles, food processing and furniture, but these were coming down in any event given that Canada was a member of GATT. The average tariff on all imports in 1950 was around 12 percent. By 1988 it had dropped to below 5 percent. Under the FTA all tariffs will be eliminated by 1998 except for a few products such as fruits and vegetables.

While tariffs have been decreasing, trade between the United States and Canada has been increasing along with jobs, output and our standard of living. In 1989 two-way trade between Canada and the United States was about $166 billion. Even though Canada's economy is only 10 percent the size of the U.S. economy, we remain their largest trading partner.[4] Over 80 percent of our exports go south of the border, making Canada the largest trading partner of the U.S.

The majority of economists agreed that Canadian firms were less efficient because of tariff protection, which encouraged too many firms to produce too many high-cost products. The result was that trade barriers, such as tariffs, led to low wages, low productivity, higher costs and low exports in manufacturing.

Second, the Mulroney government did not risk an election just to remove a few tariffs. It had bigger worries to resolve. They could be found in the rising tide of American protectionism and the development of world trading blocks. Many people in government and business worried that if Canada did not sign a free trade pact with the United States, we would have been the only industrialized country without access to a market of 100 million or more consumers. With this rising tide of U.S. protectionism in the late 1980s, the reasoning was that it was better to be in a formal North American agreement rather than outside it if and when world barriers started going up. Some may argue against such a view of international trade, but before the agreement was signed there was plenty of evidence to support it. To begin with, Canada has what economists describe as an open economy — we depend heavily on trade. From 1960 to 1985, our exports as a share of GDP increased from about 18 percent to 30 percent. These were not just raw materials and natural resources. Eighty-six percent of total merchandise exports were in manufactured goods.[5] Canada had good reason to worry about American protectionism or any program that would have affected our exports. As the U.S. trade deficit increased, so did the protectionist sentiment in their Congress. Even during the free trade talks with Canada, the United States imposed a 35 percent tariff on Canadian shakes and shingles. Clearly Canada wanted to stop the momentum of trade action, which was based not on economics but politics. A free trade agreement was one way to stop this trend. In the end the Canadian negotiators under Simon Reisman got most of what they wanted — improved access to the U.S. market.

Many critics of the deal feel that we never secured a guaranteed access to U.S. markets because Canada is still subject to current and future American trade law. If we had been exempt the United States would also have been exempt from Canada's trade law, and we would have been restricted in our ability to retaliate against unfair dumping and subsidies. But this was never a realistic or possible goal. What Mulroney's team really wanted was to rid bilateral trade of any political interference by American interest groups. This was partially achieved by negotiating a dispute settlement mechanism. Final decisions about trade disputes were now in the hands of a binational panel composed of two members from each country and a fifth member chosen jointly. Canadians now have a say in decisions previously handled only by Americans. In addition, Canadian business people now have easier movement in the United States as well as the ability to bid on equal terms with Americans for government contracts.

The third reason for the deal had to do with industrial policy. The FTA effectively binds the government's hands in supporting certain industries. For many economists, the government was doing a bad job helping out certain sectors of the economy and hampering real industrial and international adjustment. The best thing was to get the government out of the business of regional and industrial development by reducing subsidies and let the market determine what would be produced and where. This side effect of the agreement did not rest well with Canadian nationalists who believed that the government has an role, if not an obligation, to intervene directly in helping Canadian businesses. Some saw the condition of national treatment (which means both countries must not discriminate against each other's products or set limitations on investment on each other) as a clear loss in the negotiations. In any case, the FTA still allows for some flexibility to determine industrial policy, but it makes direct government intervention more difficult.[6]

As with any negotiated deal, Canada did not get everything it wanted. One of the major shortfalls was to get agreement on a definition on what constitutes a "government subsidy." To have worked out the issue during the talks would have broken down the negotiations. In order to save them, the question of subsidies was left to be worked out over a five to seven year period after the agreement went into effect. In many ways it goes to the heart of the agreement and determines how governments interact in the economy.

HOW ARE WE DOING SO FAR?

That seems to be the question on everyone's mind. The first thing to remember is that the FTA was never intended to produce instant results. Second, it will take five to ten years after the signing of the agreement before adequate study can determine the impact on jobs, output, competitiveness and productivity.[7] In the meantime we will have to be satisfied with incomplete information regardless of what some of the opponents of free trade argue. In their book, *The Free Trade Story: Faith and Fear*,[8] authors Bruce Doern and Brian Tomlin conclude that on balance Canada should benefit economically from the FTA, although they are not so sure we came out ahead politically. Other impartial evidence supports this claim. A University of Toronto study[9] based on a sophisticated model of the world economy shows that with the FTA Canada made small but positive gains in jobs, investment, lower inflation and higher exports and imports since the agreement was signed. Those conclusions were supported by another study[10] done by the Canada West Foundation, which found that exports and investments were up 6 to 7 percent in the first twenty-two months of the agreement. Any trade agreement has to be judged on whether it encourages more trade. In the first two years of the agreement, merchandise exports to America grew by 7.6 percent, while imports were up 5.1 percent.

Canada's over-all trade balance went from $14.2 billion to $17. 5 billion in our favour.[11] In terms of trade disputes the results are mixed. In the first two years, there have been eighteen. Canada won six of them compared with five won by the United States, while the rest are yet to resolved or ended in compromise.

The debate is not over yet. Figures will be distorted by supporters and opponents of the agreement to defend their cases. It is important to remember that the general movement of industrial countries is to more liberalized trade between nations, either using bilateral or multilateral agreements. As international agreements go, the FTA was modest compared with the more comprehensive one agreed to by the European Community. The FTA was never intended as a panacea to Canada's economic problems, but rather as a means to an end. Although preliminary data and theory suggest we will be better off because of the FTA, only time will tell whether we will realize the full benefits of freer trade with the United States.[12]

NOTES

[1] What's often overlooked in the free trade controversy is how modest the agreement is in its impact on the economy. An increase of a couple of percentage points in interest rates would easily swamp the benefits of the FTA in terms of jobs and output.

[2] There are those who believe that the Mulroney government made a tacit or secret deal with the Americans to keep the Canadian dollar artificially high as a condition for the United States to sign the agreement. Aside from the lack of evidence to support such a conspiracy, it's hard to imagine why anyone would agree to a condition that would prolong the recession in Canada. Besides, it would require the compliance of too many people to make it happen and therefore seems highly unlikely.

[3] One study that got considerable attention during the negotiations was done by Professor Richard Harris at Queen's University, Kingston, Ontario. He estimated that in the long run real income would rise 5 percent in Canada. In fact most economic studies showed that Canada would gain from removing barriers to trade, including reports by the Economic Council, the C.D Howe Institute, and Informetrica, an Ottawa consulting group. What most of these studies have in common is that the benefits would be positive but modest, and the gains would only be apparent in the next five to ten years.

[4] Some Canadian nationalists want us to become less dependent on the U.S. market and diversify our exports. This was tried in the late 1970s under the Third Option in the Trudeau government, but failed to increase our exports to Europe and make us less dependent on the U.S. market.

[5] Economic Council of Canada, *Changing Times*, 25th Annual Review (OECD: 1986), p. 84.

[6] The Western Provinces saw this result of the talks as victory because it prevents future federal governments from setting discriminatory export prices for energy, and therefore prevents any repeat of the National Energy Policy. As with other provisions of the agreement, this wasn't well understood. Even if an energy shortage or crisis were to arise, Canadians would be obliged to supply the United States under international energy provisions.

[7] The Canadian Labour Congress and other trade unionists claim that we have lost 350,000 jobs because of the deal with the United States. But the 1981–82 recession, a sluggish U.S. economy, and a high Canadian dollar were mainly to blame for the collapse in jobs. The 1981 recession saw almost 300,000 jobs disappear which were caused predominately by high interest rates to combat inflation. Mel Hurtig, in his book *The Betrayal of Canada* (Toronto: Stoddart, 1991) blames free trade for everything from higher unemployment and lower corporate profits to declining investments and lower merchandise trade surpluses with the U.S. To blame free trade for these problems is both simplistic and misleading.

[8] G. Bruce Doern and Brian W. Tomlin, *The Free Trade Story: Faith and Fear* (Toronto: Stoddart, 1991), p. 291.

[9] Peter Pauly, *Macroeconomic Effects of the Canada–U.S. Free Trade Agreement: An Interim Assessment* (Toronto: Institute for Policy Analysis, 1991).

[10] Diane Francis, *The Financial Post* (6 March 1991), p. 3.

[11] See *The Globe and Mail*, 9 January 1992 (letter by Michael Wilson, federal Minister of Industry, Science and Technology and International Trade).

[12] Kimberly Noble, "Box industry stands up to heavy odds," *The Globe and Mail* (7 September 1992), p. B1. One industry that has done surprisingly well since the FTA is the Canadian box industry. Instead of losing market share, this $1.5 billion industry is holding its own despite predictions by analysts that it could not survive without tariff protection.

MYTH 9
WE NEED A LOWER DOLLAR TO BE COMPETITIVE

Few points of economics confuse the layperson more than the workings of exchange rates. Nevertheless, most Canadians know that if our Canadian dollar strengthens (currency appreciation), in the sense that it can buy more U.S. currency, American products are cheaper to buy and our domestic goods are more expensive abroad. Cross-border shopping is a testimony to that simple fact. When the Canadian dollar weakens (currency depreciation) compared with the U.S. dollar, it has the opposite effect; our goods become relatively inexpensive, while the prices of imports go up. When that happens we do most of our shopping on this side of the border, and Americans start finding bargains in Canada. Based on that logic, federal government policy should seem fairly obvious: depreciate the Canadian currency by lowering its value in relation to U.S. currency. Our exports would go up; we would decrease our imports by replacing them with relatively less expensive Canadian products; and we would benefit by having more jobs all around. The balance of trade should also improve with more exports and fewer imports. It seems like the perfect solution to Canada's problems. Many businesses have been calling on the Bank of Canada to lower the Canadian dollar in the last few years (particularly those that relied on exports, such as the lumber industry) in order to restore the health of the economy. However, economic policy is not that simple. That is why it's a myth to believe that a weaker dollar will solve our balance of trade problems and increase employment.[1]

To understand what happens, let's start with how flexible exchange rates are set in the marketplace of currencies. To begin with, the price of the Canadian dollar in terms of other internationally traded currencies is determined just like any other commodity — by the forces of supply and demand. The higher the demand for the U.S. dollar, the more Canadian dollars it takes to buy it. The number of dollars available are determined primarily by the Bank of Canada. To simplify matters, over time the supply of Canadian-dollar assets are determined by the size of the government's budget. If there is a budget deficit the money supply expands, but it decreases if the budget is in surplus. The Bank of Canada can also expand or contract the supply of money if it buys or sells foreign securities with newly created Canadian-dollar bank deposits. Confusing as this may seem, the important point is that changing the demand or supply of Canadian dollars has an effect on the exchange rate just as changing the supply and demand has on the price of any good.

What determines the demand for the Canadian dollar, and hence the exchange rate? Mainly the demand for Canadian goods abroad and assets at home, such as stocks, bonds and capital investments. When the Japanese buy our coal or invest in our factories they need Canadian dollars. The same thing occurs when they buy Canadian government bonds. The greater the demand for our products, services and assets, the greater the demand for our currency. How much they buy, however, depends on the price of these goods and assets in Canadian dollars, and the exchange rate. The lower the prices are to our competitors, the more we can sell.

Another important factor to consider is the *expected* or *anticipated value* of the Canadian dollar. People and institutions hold foreign currencies not only to buy goods or earn a set return on Canadian bonds based on interest rates, but also to make money when currencies appreciate. In short, there are currency speculators who try to buy low and sell high in order to make a profit. If, for example, someone believes that the Deutsche mark is undervalued because it expects Germany's exports to increase, that speculator would buy marks today and sell when he thinks that the mark can no longer rise, or is overvalued. Sometimes speculators will nervously move billions of dollars around the globe on nothing more than a rumour, such as the medical condition of a world leader, or the anticipation of interest changes. The fact that money, because of technology, can move around the globe in seconds, twenty-four hours a day, is the most short-term and volatile factor in determining the exchange rate, and the part the press enjoys covering even though current account balances are more important in determining exchange rates over the long run.

Just as important as the above-mentioned factors is the sensitivity of the exchange rate to changes in interest rates. If interest rates on dollar assets go up, Canadians holding foreign-currency assets will switch to Canadian-dollar assets to earn a higher rate of return. Foreigners will also do the same thing. Even if interest rates change in other countries, they will have an impact on the demand for the Canadian dollar as international investors try to earn the highest rate of return on their investments.

NO SURE THING

The main way that the Canadian government influences the direction of the exchange rate is by changing the interest rate. A lower interest rate generally means less demand for Canadian-dollar assets, leading to a lower dollar. But it doesn't always work that way. From April 1990 to November 1991, the prime interest rate went from 14.75 percent down to 8.50 percent: a drop of 57.6 percent. Over the same period the Canadian dollar appreciated against the U.S. currency. In theory if capital earns less in Canada as interest rates fall, then there should be less demand for the Canadian dollar — leading to a drop or depreciation in its value. But even with a substantial drop in interest rates, that does not alway happen (see Figure 9.1). In other words, the demand for the Canadian dollar remained high. During some months, the Canadian dollar actually appreciated against the U.S. dollar while interest rates fell. The story was essentially the same for the Canadian dollar against all major currencies.

What happened? Why did demand for the Canadian dollar stay high while domestic interest rates fell? To begin with, the United States was lowering their interest rates as well, effectively frustrating and nullifying what the Canadian monetary authorities were doing, so that even if the nominal interest rates were falling in Canada the spread between the two countries was roughly the same. And it's the spread that makes all the difference. Another factor was that speculators expected stronger economic recovery in Canada and therefore bought more dollars.

Even when the Canadian dollar depreciates against the currencies of our major trading partners, that does not mean we will improve our balance of trade. A case in point is what happened to the Japanese yen in the mid 1980s. There was a spectacular depreciation of the Canadian dollar in terms of the yen from 173 yen per dollar in 1985 to 120 yen per dollar in 1986: a drop of 44 percent in the value of the dollar to the yen. One would expect a good boost of Canadian exports to Japan and a decline in imports. But that did

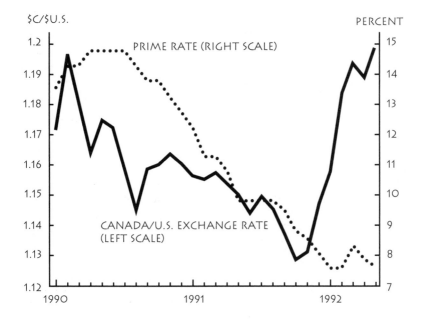

$C/$U.S.   PERCENT

Source: Bank of Canada.

FIGURE 9.1   LOW INTEREST RATES DO NOT ALWAYS MEAN A WEAKER
DOLLAR

not occur. In 1985 Canada ran deficits of $1.7 billion on our cur-
rent account (goods and services trade) with Japan. By 1986 it was
$3.9 billion, and over $4 billion in 1987.[2] To those who argue that
perhaps the dollar didn't fall far enough, the obvious question is,
how far does it have to fall? In any case, it seemed the Japanese
were getting more competitive even though their yen was getting
stronger. This was nothing new. Analysts have been saying for years
that the Japanese yen tends to improve rather than worsen Japan's
balance of trade.[3]

OTHER PROBLEMS

Even if a depreciation of the Canadian dollar means that other
countries buy more of our goods because they can afford more, it
also means that imports become more expensive. That brings us to
the next point — inflation. Canada has what is known as an open
economy, which means that exports and imports make up a large

share of GDP. For Canada it's about 30 percent. When we depreciate our currency we pay more for imported goods; and if we have to pay more for them because of a weaker, or depreciated currency, it means higher prices and more inflation.[4] That is why the governor of the Bank of Canada, who is in charge of keeping inflation down, does not like a weak dollar. That brings us back to a dilemma: a lower dollar may boost exports but does so at the expense of higher inflation and eventually higher interest rates, and no one wants that. The question is, then, what is the solution?

The answer can be partly found in the reason for the need to lower the currency in the first place, and that is to counteract the rising costs of domestic producers. If Canada's costs of production rise faster than those of our major trading partners (leading to balance of payment problems), two ways of getting back on even competitive grounds is to lower costs by raising productivity, or depreciate the value of the Canadian dollar.[5] The latter alternative is more painless in the short term. But that is a prescription for lowering our standard of living. The real test of competitiveness is not simply to sell goods on the world market and achieve balanced trade, but doing so while achieving an acceptable rate of improvement in productivity and standard of living. Trying to get an edge on the competition by depreciating currency may briefly give some relief, but if done too often other countries may end up retaliating by doing the same thing or raising tariffs. Few countries would tolerate importing someone else's unemployment simply by allowing them to cheapen their currency. In the long run, industries come to rely on less-expensive currencies as a way of avoiding the real problem of becoming more competitive through innovation and cutting costs. When Canada's merchandise trade surplus with the United States did improve, rising from $11 billion in 1982 to over $21 billion in 1985, it was because our relative cost of competitiveness was improving and not due to the devaluation of the Canadian dollar.[6]

The U.S. economy suffered the same problem as Canada during the last decade. Since 1986 the U.S. dollar has been lower against most foreign currencies than it was in 1980; but at the beginning of the 1980s the United States exported more manufacturing goods than it imported. During the late 1980s it found itself running deficits of over $100 billion. Why didn't the lower dollar help? The answer, in short, is that the United States just wasn't as competitive as it had once been.[7]

The trick for Canada is to take a page from Japan's and Germany's book. Both of these countries were able to maintain balance of payment surpluses throughout the 1980s even though their currencies underwent remarkable appreciations during that decade. How did they manage to do it when other countries couldn't? The simple answer is that they made goods the world wanted at any price, such as cars, electronics and consumer products. That was their key to an improved standard of living: to maintain market share regardless of whether prices are going up. There are no quick remedies, such as getting rich by depreciating a nation's currency. The Japanese and Germans relied on product innovation rather than devalued currencies to improve their productivity and competitiveness.

NOTES

1 The corollary to this myth is that a strong dollar means a strong economy. Just as a lower dollar doesn't guarantee more exports and fewer imports, a strong dollar policy has little to do with a healthy economy.

2 *Bank of Canada Review*, December 1990, p. 119.

3 Robert Solomon, *The International Monetary System, 1945–1981* (Harper & Row 1982), p. 359.

4 What if prices or the rate of inflation differ from one country to another? Under a fixed exchange rate system, one country can import another's inflation. This is not so, theoretically, under a flexible exchange rate system. If prices rise faster in Mexico than Canada, we will buy fewer Mexican products, while our products become relatively cheaper. Flexible exchange rates provide a buffer or mechanism where one country can protect itself from importing another country's inflation. Flexible rates are also a way to keep balance of payments in equilibrium between countries. If German producers are more competitive, their cost of production falls, which means higher exports and less imports. As they run a balance of trade surplus, other countries such as Canada import more and export less, which means we have a balance of trade deficit. As countries buy fewer Canadian products, their demand for the Canadian dollars to buy our goods falls, which triggers a depreciation in the Canadian dollar, which in turn makes our products cheaper to buy. The depreciation of the Canadian dollar, or appreciation of the German mark, carries the seed of their own reversal.

5 In this respect Canada hasn't performed well. Between 1981 and 1988, the U.S. Bureau of Labour Statistics data show that output per hour in Canadian manufacturing rose 2.3 percent per year, the lowest rate of increase among the seven major OECD countries. In relation to the United States, Canada's major trading

partner, labour cost performance was also disappointing. Unit labour costs rose on average 3 percent per year over the 1980s compared to only 0.4 percent in the United States. Similar data also show that between 1979 and 1985, Canada had the worst performance in the growth of output per person and total factor productivity. See Statistics Canada, *Perspectives*, Summer 1990, pp. 10–12.

[6]   *Perspectives*, pp. 9–10.

[7]   Paul Krugman, *The Age of Diminished Expectations* (Cambridge, Mass.: MIT Press, 1990), p. 97.

'BUY CANADIAN' MEANS MORE JOBS

"Buy the cars your neighbours build" became a popular slogan for the Canadian Auto Workers when the domestic auto industry began losing market share to the Japanese. The argument seems to make sense. Buying cars from Windsor or Oshawa does provide jobs for Canadian workers. But should it be used as an argument for restricting imports? The answer is a clear no.

Few myths die harder than the notion that "if we produce it in Canada, we'll keep the jobs," and few economic arguments have less validity. This variant of the anti-trade position that "we can't compete with inexpensive labour," is equally as fallacious as the idea that "we can't compete with inexpensive imports." These arguments still have appeal today even though many of their kind have been discredited over the centuries.[1] Just like any justification to protect domestic industry, it is usually couched in helping the interests of the nation when in fact it is protecting the interests of a particular industry or labour group.

On the surface Buy Canadian policies appear to make sense, but digging below the surface reveals that the argument doesn't hold. To begin with, if the argument applies to the auto industry, why not to all industries? After all, by keeping all imports out we can produce everything here, keeping all the jobs for ourselves. To carry the analogy one step further, why not protect Ontario grape growers from British Columbia farmers? If that sounds absurd, it is exactly what interprovincial trade barriers were doing before we slowly started taking them down.[2] In the end, keeping out imports under the guise of protecting jobs at home leads to higher prices and a lower standard of living.

When a country decides to use tariffs to protect a given sector of the economy from foreign competition it is, in effect, redistributing income from one sector of the economy to another. As we've seen in Chapters 5 and 8, the tariffs turn out to be an expensive way of protecting jobs and distributing income[3]. Buy Canadian policies have the same effect by appealing to our sense of nationalism.

Argentina is a perfect case of what can happen when special interests sabotage trade and competition policy. Half a century ago Argentina and Canada both had promising economic futures. Since then Argentina has neared collapse under a massive misallocation of resources, high unemployment, crippling budget and trade deficits, loss of investment, and hyperinflation in which prices rose an annual average of 450 percent throughout the 1980s. By 1990, what was one of the richest nations on earth sixty years ago, had a GDP per capita that was 10 percent of the OECD average. It is not hard to see what happened. Governments channelled resources into unproductive sectors, while import barriers protected inefficient industries. It was no secret that powerful trade unions, no competition and runaway budget deficits made it impossible to check inflation. Now Argentina is scrambling to open its markets to competition and undo the damage of decades of protectionist economic policies.[4]

Another problem with restricting imports to encourage employment is that other countries will not stand idly by taking our exports while we restrict theirs. Before long everyone starts implementing these beggar-my-neighbour policies. In the end, it makes everyone worse off. That is what happened during the Great Depression of the 1930s as countries tried to export their unemployment by keeping imports out. But we don't have to go back sixty years to see the effects of these policies. Every time there is a recession or surge in imports, governments come under pressure to protect jobs and companies by restricting these imports.[5] That is exactly what is happening in the case of grain production. Canada cannot sell its wheat because too many countries are busy protecting their grain farmers, even though Canadian producers are among the most efficient in the world.

THE NEW MERCANTILISM

The desire to restrict imports comes from the basic notion that imports are bad and exports are good. Despite the obvious drawbacks in the impulse to keep imports out, there is no denying that policies to protect domestic companies from competition do provide immediate (if not lasting) relief. It seems to make sense that if we buy a Japanese car, we get the car but they get the money; but if we buy Canadian, we get the car and the money as well. This is an extension of mercantilism, the sixteenth-century philosophy that European colonies should be used mainly for exporting to and not importing from. Therefore, according to this notion, a country should always strive for a positive balance of trade (exports exceed imports). But such a policy is illogical. We can always sell more goods by lowering the price of exported goods, subsidizing those industries that export, or devaluing the currency. But should we? Do exporters need subsidies because they belong to some under-privileged group? If we encourage exports by pricing below the cost of production, Canadians end up subsidizing foreign buyers. No one would argue that American consumers should be encouraged to benefit at the Canadian taxpayers' expense. But that's exactly what happens when we make our exports less expensive than they would normally be without subsidies. There is another problem as well: the higher export subsidies are, the higher the profits in the export sector will be, which means that more resources will be taken out of domestic production resulting in a misallocation of resources from domestic products to exports.

Another misconception about increasing exports at the expense of imports, is that when we buy imported goods, other countries then hold Canadian dollars. Mexicans or Germans don't hold Canadian dollars for the pleasure of holding them but for buying Canadian goods when they want them. We demand foreign currency for the same reasons. In the long run a country's exports are determined by how much it imports; otherwise, how would we get paid? If we restrict the buying of imported goods, other countries end up with fewer dollars to buy *our* exports. The greater the exports we want, the more we have to import and vice-versa.

In simple terms, the process of adjustments works as follows. A Canadian vintner delivers a shipment of wines to an importer in Britain who pays for the shipment in British pounds. But the Canadian wine maker can't pay his Canadian suppliers and labour with any currency other than Canadian funds. Where does he get it? The answer is, from a build-up in Canadian dollar credits from British exports to Canada. In other words, if it weren't for imports from Britain, the British would not have been able to import the wine from Canada. Foreign exchange is a clearing transaction in which British pounds and Canadian-dollar credits are cancelled against each other. There is no mystery about it. On a more immediate and local level, each of us must sell something, even if it's our own labour, in order to have purchasing power. Just as internal trade is conducted by cancelling cheques through bank clearing houses, the same process applies in international trade.

This is obviously an oversimplification of the complex rules that govern international trade, but the basic principle holds: if we want to export more, we have to import more. If a country runs a trade deficit for too long, it restricts its long-run ability to import indefinitely. But even running surpluses brings its own problems. The Japanese have run up enormous foreign exchange reserves credits over the years, and now they are under pressure to use them.[6] It is not that the Japanese have been overexporting, but underconsuming foreign goods. One way or another those credits will be run down[7] because they cannot be used to buy domestic products.[8]

VARIATION ON A THEME: MANUFACTURING MATTERS

Despite the various and discredited arguments for protecting domestic producers, new arguments are always being created to defend the indefensible. The latest version falls under the category that "manufacturing matters" and therefore must be protected with import restrictions if necessary.

The argument goes something like this: Western nations are undergoing a process of deindustrialization in which services are replacing manufacturing as the dominant source of economic activity. Those who advocate this position claim that a modern society cannot sustain a service-driven economy without manufacturing. Stephen Cohen and John Zysman, who advocate protection on this assumption, state that "there are...other kinds of linkages in the economy, such as those which tie the crop duster to the cotton fields, the ketchup maker to the tomato patch, the wine press to the vineyards. Here the linkages are tight and quite concrete."[9]

What this means is that if a country loses one link in the production process, it jeopardizes all the links. But if one takes a quick look at how things are made in a world that is becoming more integrated (and not less), the opposite is true. It's not unusual to have a garment designed on Queen Street in Toronto with cotton grown in the Southern United States, cut in Hong Kong and sold in London.[10] According to Cohen and Zysman, anything to do with cotton should be done in the southern United States.

DUMPING AND PREDATOR PRICING

If buying Canadian isn't a good enough argument for keeping out imports, perhaps one should look at imports that are sold at below the cost of production or at lower prices than those offered in the home market. This is one case where government intervention is justified. Dumping is universally condemned, and it is the only time that GATT allows countries to defend themselves with special tariffs. However dumping *alone* is not viewed as sufficient reason for countervailing duties. In Canada, for example, it must be shown after study by the Department of National Revenue that material harm has been done to the domestic industry, otherwise no protection is allowed. In most cases the government decides to monitor the situation. If little or no harm is done, then dumping is a bargain for the importing country. Although the situation can't be allowed to go on forever, the practice is not always condemned, especially when the consumer is the winner.

Predator pricing is a different situation. The objective of the producer is to drive the price low enough to eliminate competition and to increase market share, with the purpose of extracting higher prices later on. The most adamant free-marketer would not justify such practices, even if consumers were to benefit for a short time. The cost of adjustment to the companies and workers affected are usually greater than any benefits that consumers receive. In such cases, governments should do what they can to prevent expensive disruptions to their markets.[11]

When all arguments for greater protection are dismissed by logic and reason, Buy Canadian policies are defended on the grounds of national pride and honour. Even the federal government has been running ads encouraging us to check labels to make sure we are buying Canadian. It may make good politics but it's bad economics. We are reproached, on the basis of our fellowship with other Canadians, for allowing other countries to provide us with the necessities of life. Just listen to the farmers trying to protect the marketing boards or the auto workers defending their jobs. When unions and industry appeal to your sense of nationalism on the grounds that it protects jobs, it's time for consumers to watch their wallets.

WHAT IS TO BE DONE?

It has to be recognized that justifications for protectionism are few and far between, and that governments should resist calls to protect certain workers or firms at the expense of the consumer. That does not mean that governments are helpless to provide protection and relief to the import-sensitive industries and their workers. Help should come in the form of adjustment assistance and retraining programs that anticipate and encourage change with well-thought-out programs. The bulk of assistance should come from the proper management of monetary and fiscal policy that steers the economy to fuller employment. Canadian consumers would be doing themselves and their country a favour if they bought goods and services based on price and quality rather than if they are Canadian or not. This also applies to government procurement policies. Otherwise we all end up poorer.

NOTES

[1] Over a century ago the French economist Frederic Bastiat satirized the French candle makers for asking the government to protect them from the sun's light by passing a law forcing everyone to shutter their windows, dormers and skylights. They argued that during the day the sun's cost of production was zero, and they certainly couldn't compete at those prices. See Blomqvist, Wonnacott and Wonnacott, *Economics*, 1st Cdn. ed. (Scarborough: McGraw-Hill Ryerson, 1983), p. 632.

[2] Within Canada, until 1992, Canadian beer could only be sold in the province where it was brewed. That led to the absurd anomaly that a Canadian brand such as Moosehead could be found in New York but not Toronto.

[3] Policies to protect jobs in the United States were even more expensive for society. One study concluded that trade protection in thirty-one industries cost consumers $53 billion in 1984. Protecting a single job in autos cost $105,000; in television manufacturing $420,000; and $750,000 for every job saved in the steel industry. See Gary Hufbauer *et al.*, *Trade Protection in the United States: 31 Case Studies* (Washington, D.C.: Institute for International Economics, 1986).

⁴ See "Nearly Time to Tango," *The Economist*, 18 April 1992, p. 17.

⁵ Opposition to imports comes not only from organized labour and some industries but also from the Canadian Conference of Catholic Bishops, which has come out against labour-destroying technology and an industrial policy to encourage labour-intensive manufacturing. That position is reminiscent of the Luddites who destroyed the textile machines for the same reason in eighteenth-century England. The truth is, technology isn't the destroyer of jobs, and manufacturing can only remain competitive if it uses labour-saving technology. Otherwise the only way to maintain employment, and only in the short run, is to limit imports. That puts the bishops in the awkward position of favouring jobs for Canadian workers at the expense of jobs abroad, and often in countries with higher levels of unemployment. See Gregory Baum and Duncan Cameron, "Ethical Reflections on the Economic Crises," *Ethics and Economics* (Toronto: James Lorimer and Company, 1984), p. 185.

⁶ It's important to realize that trade surpluses aren't a sign of a healthy economy. Some countries that ran surpluses in recent years were Poland, Venezuela, Hungary, Mexico, Gabon and Chile.

⁷ That's one reason Japanese companies such as Sony have been investing heavily in the United States, to buy Columbia Pictures for $3.4 billion U.S. in 1989, and Matsushita's $6 billion U.S. purchase of MCA. In 1987, Honda set up operations in the United States in order to export 50,000 cars back to Japan.

⁸ The argument will inevitably arise that the Japanese are unfair traders for not allowing others into their markets, coupled with government incentives to help their export sector. This is a contentious issue because most of the evidence to support this view is anecdotal. But Japan's tariffs are among the lowest in the world, and economic studies are inconclusive at best that Japan is unfairly keeping out imports. See Jagdish Bhagwati, *Protectionism* (Cambridge, Mass.: MIT Press, 1988) p. 69.

⁹ Stephen Cohen and John Zysman, *Manufacturing Matters: The Myth of the Post-Industrial Economy* (New York: Basic Books, 1987).

¹⁰ The famous international economist Jagdish Bhagwati was amused as he read these lines while eating some British Crabtree and Evelyn vintage marmalade. "It surely never occurred to me that England grew its own oranges." See *Protectionism*, p. 114.

¹¹ What about the situation in which countries, such as Japan, price their products abroad at lower prices than they charge at home? On the face of it, this isn't always dumping or justification for imposing countervailing duties. Firms always charge a lower price in markets where the competition is greater. That is usually the case when Japanese cameras and camcorders are cheaper here than in Japan. We do not have to go to the Far East to find examples. The "grey market" is an example of how firms charge different prices in different markets. Office products, computer disks, batteries and film are products that companies ship at various prices around the world. The problem arises when grey marketeers make a profit by buying in one country and shipping to another market where prices are higher. This technique is called "arbitrage" and companies fight hard to prevent it, though it's usually tough to stop.

MYTH 11

IMMIGRANTS STEAL JOBS FROM CANADIANS

One of the more common myths heard in Canada is that immigrants steal jobs from Canadians and reduce their wages, especially during times of high unemployment and economic slowdown. The implications of more immigration are obvious: more immigration means there is less to go around for the rest of us native-born Canadians. Those who hold this view also tend to believe that immigrants are a burden to the taxpayer because new Canadians are seen to be using more than their share of unemployment insurance, welfare and other social programs. A more sophisticated criticism is that too many immigrants reduce the per capita income of residents in the country. This is based on the assumption that there is an optimal population size and that beyond some point, the economy isn't as efficient; and, therefore, per capita income starts falling. Finally, it is thought, this problem will only get worse if Canada continues its liberal policy of increasing the range of immigration as it has been since the 1960s.

Given that Canada is a land where immigration has played a crucial role in economic development, there is surprisingly little information about its social and economic impact. But from what we know, do immigrants steal jobs, reduce our income, and take more from the system than they contribute? The answer, on all counts, is no. All the techniques of economic analysis cannot find a bit of evidence that immigration has adverse effects on the employment and earnings of Canadians. Before we examine the available evidence in more detail, let's take a look at the changing role and history of immigration in Canada.

THE CHANGING FACE OF IMMIGRATION

Canada has always been known as a country of immigrants but during the latter part of the last century, Canada actually had more people leaving than arriving. Immigration reached the astounding number of 401,000 new immigrants in 1913, but only 25 percent of those who came stayed. The rest went to the United States. There was another net loss of people in the 1930s and early 1940s, but after that things started to pick up. From 1946 to 1957, 1.1 million immigrants arrived. They came mainly from Europe and mainly for the purpose of finding better jobs and higher wages. Those who arrived in this wave often had few skills, but did have a desire to work hard. After 1957 Canada changed its immigration focus by recruiting those with skills or money. By the late 1960s, professionals made up 25 percent of all immigrants. With the adoption of the point system, Canada emphasized skills and education and downplayed immigrant sponsorship. The countries from which immigrants came also began to change with the new rules for entry. Before the 1960s over 85 percent of all immigrants came from either Europe or the United States. By the late 1960s and early 1970s, 40 percent arrived from the West Indies, the Middle East, Asia and Africa.[1] The face of Canada was transformed: it was no longer predominately white and European. The English and French Canadians were now minorities in their own country.

BURDEN OR BLESSING?

Now that we have this rough backdrop to the question of immigration, what has been its impact on the Canadian economy? To help answer this question, we can look at immigration in three ways: first, its contribution to the per capita income of native-born Canadians (or those already living in Canada); second, the immigrants' use of federal and provincial social programs in relation to taxes paid; and third, the question as to whether immigrants actually create work or displace Canadians from jobs, thereby raising the rate of unemployment.

Economic Efficiency

The question of economic efficiency centres around the idea that there's some ideal or optimal level of population, and that after that has been reached, per capita income levels begin to drop. Economists call this the law of diminishing marginal returns. This economic law simply means that the more people there are, the less contribution the last one makes to national output.[2] There comes a point when, regardless of how many people are added, output and income won't go up any further. In fact it may actually decrease as population grows. That is what we mean by reaching our maximum efficiency point. Have we reached that point? The answer is, no — and we probably never will. Economists like to have fun trying to figure out some optimum population point where adding any more people would make the economy work less efficiently. One estimate by the Economic Council of Canada puts Canada's optimal population size at 100 million, but that is only sophisticated guess work.[3] Besides, output depends on more than just how many workers there are. Machines, tools and technology are also important and those inputs are always changing, making labour more productive. That is why there is no clear relationship between population size and economic efficiency.

Social Programs and Taxes

Another important question deals with the dependence of immigrants on welfare and other social assistance programs. A common perception is that immigrants use the system more than native-born Canadians. The data shows that 12.5 percent of the immigrants that arrived between 1981 and 1986 used the welfare system compared with 13.8 percent of native-born Canadians. Among those who immigrated to Canada from 1976 to 1980, only 6.7 percent were on welfare. It seems the longer immigrants are in Canada, the less they rely on welfare. Contrary to conventional wisdom, only a small share of immigrants ever go on welfare, and certainly no more than native-born Canadians.

It would follow that if immigrants do not overuse the welfare system, they must have jobs to go to; and in fact they do. Immigrants in general have lower unemployment rates than Canadians born in the country. For 1986 immigrants had an unemployment rate of 8.2 percent compared to 10.8 percent for nonimmigrants. (But recent immigrants to the country did have higher rates of unemployment as they adjusted to their new country.)

Do immigrants pay their fair share of taxes, or do they use more social services than they pay for? One study has found that immigrants do indeed pay more in taxes than they take out in services. In short, immigrants carry more than their share of costs and in the process transfer income through their taxes to native-born Canadians. The study further found that the younger the immigrant, the higher their contribution. By paying taxes, the immigrant makes a net contribution to society for up to thirty-five years. The implication is that if we are going to bring in immigrants, then we should do it when they are young.[4] Another plus is that in 1986, 27.5 percent of adult immigrants who had to qualify under the point system to gain entry into the country entered with university degrees, saving taxpayers considerable educational expense. This compares to 22.6 percent of native-born Canadians who earned university degrees.

If immigrants make a positive financial contribution to the country, why not let more come into the country? The case has been made that as the Canadian population ages, the country will need more workers to pay for the soaring costs in health, education and social security. The Economic Council of Canada has found that we can reduce the per capita tax burden of administering these services per person if we have higher immigration levels. But these savings would be very small.[5] Even if we add the benefits of economies of scale, in other words the reduced per capita costs of a higher population, the benefits to the host population would still be small. What the evidence seems to show is that immigrants do not pose a burden to the host population in higher taxes, but they also do not substantially alleviate the tax burden to the rest of the population either.

It would be wrong to assume that immigration, including refugees looking for asylum in Canada, does not have its social and economic costs. In 1985 all levels of government spent $432 million on programs for immigrants ranging from language training and social assistance to counselling and job placement. But these costs, which have been rising with the increase in immigration and refugee status claims, do not capture the added burden on the three major destinations of immigrants (Toronto, Montreal and Vancouver) in terms of higher housing and social costs caused by growth in population. Immigration has not been a national phenomenon, but one highly focussed on Canada's three major urban centres.

Jobs, Income and Immigrants

Now we come to the belief that immigrants steal our jobs. People who believe immigrants displace native-born Canadians base their reasoning on three assumptions: first, that immigrants displace jobs on a one-to-one basis; second, that immigrant and native-born labour are perfectly interchangeable; and third, that immigrants are willing to work at lower wages than host Canadians. Such assumptions are usually not based on evidence but on the view that there are a fixed number of jobs in the economy. We know this isn't true by the fact that as the population grows through immigration, the demand for goods and services increases along with the demand for new jobs. In many ways immigrants create their own jobs and increase the level of aggregate demand by buying cars, houses, and everything else that Canadians purchase. But we do know that recent immigrants spend a higher portion of their income on food, shelter and transportation, and because of their spending patterns, change the nature of aggregate demand in the economy. On the supply side, immigrants also tend to contribute more to the labour force. When adjusted for age, the 1981 participation rate for male immigrants was 79.4 percent compared to 77.9 percent for nonimmigrants. And where once Canada gave preference to immigrants with technical skills that were in short supply domestically, there's a greater tendency today for immigrants to find jobs in professional and administrative occupations.

In reference to the idea that immigrants are willing to work at jobs refused by Canadians, this view sees the economy having primary and secondary jobs, the first being high-paying ones preferred by native-born Canadians, and the latter poorer-paying jobs preferred by immigrants. This black and white approach to the labour market is flawed because it depends too much on assumptions that are unfounded. For example, if native-born Canadians did not want to work in secondary jobs, it would soon become apparent — farmers, for example, wouldn't get their crops picked, houses would go uncleaned and lawns unmowed. In a market economy, a labour shortage would dictate that wages in these secondary occupations would go up. There is no theoretical reason why native-born Canadians wouldn't work in these occupations. A possible explanation would be that immigrants possess many of the same skills as the native-born population. As the number of immigrants increases they compete for the same number of jobs at lower wage rates. This is a possible scenario, but there is no evidence to support it. If this were the case, wages for native-born Canadians would drop. But there's no evidence that this happens. Immigration does not seem to affect the wages of native-born Canadians.[6] This can be partly explained by the fact that immigrants and native-born Canadians are not perfect substitutes or completely interchangeable. How immigrants and native-born Canadians interact economically is not well understood and needs more investigation and research. The skills of immigrants vary greatly among and between the immigrants themselves and their countries of origin. Persons migrating under one set of economic and political conditions have different impacts in the labour market; and it is difficult, if not impossible, to tell what these impacts will be beforehand.

Even though the evidence suggests that immigration does not increase unemployment, the federal government acted as if it did by reducing target levels of immigration during recessions. Until 1990, under the point system an immigrant could not apply for landed immigrant status, other than under the family unification program, unless there was a need for their occupation. Although it might appear to the layperson that it would be an easy matter to deter-

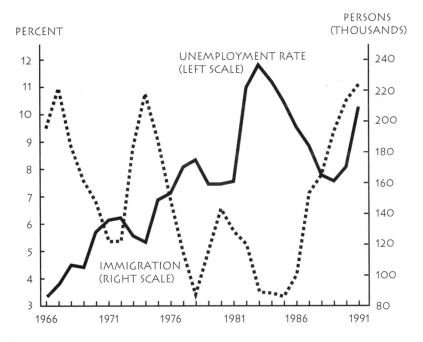

Source: StatsCan.

FIGURE 11.1   RELATIONSHIP OF IMMIGRATION TO AVAILABLE EMPLOYMENT

mine whether immigration causes unemployment to rise, in reality it is not all that straightforward. The Department of Employment and Immigration has looked at this question from various angles to find the answer. Simply looking at the data and seeing if unemployment rates increase with immigration levels is unsatisfying. It isn't enough to look at immigration flows to see whether the unemployment rates go up or down. A quick examination of the data shows that immigration tapers off as the unemployment rate increases. After all, immigrants generally do not want to come here unless there are jobs waiting (see Figure 11.1).

A cursory examination of the data does not tell us much about what is going on underneath the numbers. If we assume that immigration is just another way of increasing population size, we might find a relationship between unemployment and the population increases; however, no such correlation can be found between the two.[7] Another way to increase unemployment may be to increase the labour force beyond the capacity of the economy to produce jobs, but do countries with high labour force growth rates have higher levels of unemployment? Comparing the experience of various OECD countries, again there is no relationship between unemployment rates and the growth of the labour force. Canada had a lower unemployment rate than France and Italy in the late 1980s even though our labour force grew at a faster pace.

Another supporting piece of evidence that immigrants do not cause more unemployment is that they tend to create their own jobs through self-employment. In 1981, 7.9 percent of immigrants were self-employed compared to 6.8 percent of Canadians. For 1986, the comparable numbers were 11.6 percent and 9 percent; self-employment grew faster among immigrants than the general population. Finally there is the question of who fares better under our immigration policy. Again there is the problem of inadequate information and data. On average, immigrants not only have jobs to go to, but also tend to earn more than native-born Canadians — about 3 percent more, adjusting for factors such as educational levels.

What we conclude from the studies and analyses of immigration in Canada is that first, immigrants do not steal jobs; second, there's no evidence that immigrants lower the earnings of native-born Canadians; and third, immigrants are not a burden on the welfare system. Finally, immigrants pay more than their fair share of taxes for social programs. But if there's no evidence that they are a burden to society, it should also be said that there are no compelling reasons for assuming that immigrants are either good or bad for the native-born population in terms of increasing per capita income. This means that to understand the costs and benefits of immigration, one has to look beyond economics and assess the contributions of a society that has a diverse mix of cultures and provides a haven on humanitarian grounds. But if anyone persists in believing that immigrants steal jobs, they can not count on the evidence to make their case.

NOTES

1   Immigrants can enter Canada in three main ways: through family unification, as independents, or as refugees. From 1980 to 1986, 43.1 percent came into Canada by way of family-class immigration; 18.3 percent were refugees; and 40 percent came into the country as independents. About 70 percent of the refugees and family-class immigrants come from the Caribbean, Asia, Africa, South and Central America, while 50 percent of the independents came from traditional sources of immigration such as the United Kingdom, Europe, and the United States.

2   The law of diminishing marginal returns assumes that as more people are added, the output of the next person added is less than the previous after a certain point. This assumes that there is no increase in capital, land or other factors of production. If there is only so much machinery to work with, the output of the next worker will not be as great as the previous one.

3   Economic and Social Impacts of Immigration by the Economic Council of Canada (Ottawa: Supply and Services, 1991).

4   Ather H. Akbari, "The Benefits of Immigration to Canada: Evidence on Tax and Public Services," Canadian Public Policy, XV, no.4, December 1989.

5   Economic Council of Canada, Economic and Social Impacts of Immigration, p. 51.

6   For U.S. data, it was found that the impact on native-born American earnings was negligible. A 10 percent increase in immigration decreased native-born American earnings by 0.2 percent. For manufacturing workers it was a mere 0.04 percent. Even the impact of illegal Mexican labour hardly affects the earnings of native-born Americans. See George J. Borjas, Friends or Strangers (New York: Basic Books 1990).

7   Economic Council of Canada, Economic and Social Impacts of Immigration, p. 54.

THE GOVERNMENT CAN'T AFFORD AN AGING POPULATION

A common anxiety today is the notion that governments can't afford an aging population given the tremendous demands put on the nation's limited resources. The scenario goes something like this: as the baby boom generation gets older and begins to retire, and as the generation following behind it shrinks, in size, there will be fewer people contributing to the tax base. Not only will more people be retiring as a proportion of the population, but also they will be living longer; and as everyone knows, the older we get the more medical attention we need. Eventually, the government will go bankrupt trying to pay out all health, retirement and social insurance programs. Fewer workers will be supporting more retirees. By the time the baby boom generation leaves the labour market, there won't even be enough money around to cover the old age pension. In short, "the government can't afford an aging population." Little wonder that many are happy to bail out now while there's something left in the government coffers.

Before we examine this fallacy, let's be clear that governments do not go broke in the conventional sense, at least not the way companies or individuals do. There is the erroneous notion that if households have to live within their means, so then do governments. With individuals, if you spend more than you earn, your creditors can force the sale of your assets to pay off your debts. That's what we normally mean by going broke or becoming insolvent. Those who believe that governments must behave as individuals and balance their budgets are committing the error of *fallacy of composition*: what applies to the parts applies to the whole. But this is not so with governments because they have the power to change the law. If they need more money to pay their bills, all they have to do is borrow, raise taxes, or if they are really desperate, print more money. They also don't have a definite lifetime over which to balance their budgets. Governments only go broke in the sense that they cannot meet their obligations from current revenues. A helpful illustration for that point is the problem that occurred with countries such as Brazil and Mexico after they went on borrowing binges in the 1970s. They couldn't meet interest payments on loans from foreign lenders so the only real option left to the lenders was to refuse to extend further credit to delinquent nations. Often, however, the creditor nations lent more money when they couldn't make payments so that their capital markets wouldn't be thrown into disarray. No one can force a country, short of going to war, to liquidate assets to pay their bills. Therefore, countries don't *truly* "go broke."

It's true that more Canadians will be exiting the labour force over the next twenty years. A simple look at the demographics tells the story. Those between the ages of forty-five and sixty-four accounted for 20 percent of the population in 1986, but will account for 28 percent in 2011. Over the next fifty years the proportion of the population age sixty-five and over will double. Coupled with this greying of Canada will be a shrinking labour force. There will be only slightly more young people around in 2001 than there were in 1991. As we get older and begin to retire en masse, this aging population group will be collecting federal Canada pensions, old age security benefits and guaranteed income supplement payments. We can also expect greater demands for health care dollars. It is assumed that the entire system will come crashing down around us as we get older, sicker and poorer. But is that distressing scenario inevitable? For the following reasons, probably not: markets react to changes in demographics by substituting more capital for labour; the labour force won't necessarily continue to shrink indefinitely; and technology will most likely continue to advance as it always does.

CAPITAL WILL REPLACE LABOUR

It's true that as the labour force shrinks as a share of the population, so does the tax base from which the government draws its revenues. But economic wealth and growth also depends on physical and human capital, or the tools with which we do our work. Physical capital includes machinery, buildings, equipment, dams, bridges and so on. Human capital is made up of all accumulated knowledge and skills of a working population. These are what

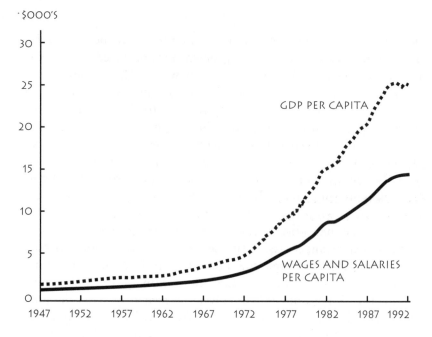

· $000'S

30

25

GDP PER CAPITA

20

15

10

5

WAGES AND SALARIES
PER CAPITA

0

1947   1952   1957   1962   1967   1972   1977   1982   1987 1992

Source: StatsCan.

FIGURE 12.1   FEWER WORKERS DO NOT ALWAYS MEAN A POORER SOCIETY

economists call inputs. As the labour force shrinks the demand for labour will increase and with it the returns to labour in higher wages and salaries. As labour becomes more expensive, there will be more capital-labour substitution. In fact, the more capital we have, the more productive we become. That's why Canada's GDP per capita has risen faster than wages and salaries (see Figure 12.1). It's productivity, or output per worker, that's key to improving a country's standard of living. The more productive the economy, the larger the wealth base for the government to tax in order to meet growing expenditures. Sustaining a steady productivity growth level over a long period of time is the key to success. The irony is that a shrinking labour force may actually make us better off by forcing the economy to become more capital intensive and more productive. This is what happened to Japan's economy in the late 1940s when its population experienced lower fertility rates. Japan began to run out of workers twenty years before the United States and Canada. Some economists have argued that it was this labour shortage that forced Japan to turn to machines to do their work, which led to Japan's phenomenal productivity growth rates that averaged over 10 percent a year for almost twenty years after 1945.

If our wealth and future well-being are actually measured by our productivity, how does Canada fare? We are one of the winners. Since 1950, we've increased our real (taking inflation into account) income per capita from $ 6,000 to $22,000 by 1990. But we could have done better. During the 1960s and early 1970s our rate of productivity growth averaged close to 5 percent per year. If we had maintained that growth rate until 1990, we could have added another $160 billion to our gross domestic product thanks to the miracle of compound growth. Although our productivity levels have been disappointing, there are indications that the end of the low productivity rates of the 1970s and 1980s may be behind us.[1] Since 1987, Canada has experienced a boom in capital investment and formation, which means that labour has more capital to work with. Investment in machinery and equipment increased by over 100 percent from in the early 1980s to $47 billion in 1989.

If we want more capital and productivity, how do we get it? Here, economists have a standard reply: *sacrifice*. Consume less today so we'll have more tomorrow. The more a country saves, the more funds available for investment.[2] Canadians have traditionally been good savers, and with the added incentives of retirement savings plans (RSPs) we're salting away billions of dollars. A lot of these funds are in the hands of older people, which has the added benefit that as the proportion of the population covered by private pensions and RSPs increases, the pressure for public assistance programs should decrease.

AN OLDER POPULATION DOES NOT MEAN A SMALLER WORK FORCE

The second assumption implied by this myth is that the labour force will shrink or become stagnant as the baby boom "bulge" works its way through the system. This is not necessarily the case. As we've already seen, a shrinking labour force means higher wages, which also implies that a greater number of older workers will want to keep working. Currently, those sixty-five years and over who are still working make up only about 15 percent of the Canadian labour force. Comparable figures in Germany are 22 percent, with 23 percent in the United Kingdom, 18 percent in the United States and over 26 percent in Sweden. It won't take much to increase Canada's labour force as more people choose to remain in the work force longer in order to provide for their own old age. Older, more experienced workers, who remain in the labour market longer, are more productive and valuable than younger workers.

If the past is any indication, women will also be entering the labour force in greater numbers. Over the past decade, women have increased their participation rate to almost 60 percent, while that rate for men has remained roughly constant at 75 percent. Today more and more married women are joining the labour force to the point where single-earner couples are in the minority. One incentive for women to continue entering the labour market will be there as wages go up.

Another obvious way to increase the supply of workers is through immigration. The government can turn the immigration flow on and off as required. For example, in 1989 the number of immigrants was about 189,000 compared to only 85,000 in 1985. Canada's population has been increasing despite the fact that we are having fewer children. In 1960, Canadians had about 4 children per family. By the late 1980s, we had fewer than 1.6 children, a number below the 2.1 average per family needed to replace the population. If we assume current fertility rates and 200,000 immigrants a year, the Canadian population won't peak until the 2030s. Just because Canada's natural population growth rate is low, doesn't necessarily mean a static or shrinking population or labour force.

TECHNOLOGY'S MANY SURPRISES

"The government can't afford an aging population" theme makes one more crucial, but erroneous, assumption and that is that technology will somehow remain stagnant, or at best won't contribute to the economy. No one can predict how technology advancements will improve productivity, but there's a strong link between research and development and technology, productivity and economic well-being. Who could have predicted the impact of microelectronics, genetic engineering, and materials (i.e., ceramics and plastics) research thirty years ago? Ignoring the dynamics of technological advances led to the faulty reasoning at the turn of the century about the massive shift of workers out of agriculture and to manufacturing. The contention then was that if workers left the fields for the factories, there would be no one to grow the food to feed everyone moving to the cities. What many didn't take into account were the

giant strides occurring in agricultural technology, which transformed agriculture into one of the most productive sectors in the
country. At the turn of the century almost half of the adult working
population was in agriculture. Today, that number is around 4 percent and there is no shortage of food production in sight.

BUT DON'T THE OLD GET SICKER?

Perhaps one of the more compelling arguments about the standard
of living declining as a greater share of the population retires, is the
argument about the rising costs of medical care for the elderly. After
all, the elderly consume a greater share of medical dollars compared
to those in their twenties and thirties. Health care makes up
Canada's biggest, single social program. But unlike the United
States, Canada was able to bring health care costs under control
and prevented a cost explosion with the introduction of a universal
health care program. Canada spends about 8 percent of its national
income on health care compared to 11 percent in the United States.
But can we prevent a cost explosion in medical care as we get older?
The evidence suggests we can.

A lot of serious thought has gone into this very question.
After all, it is central to how governments spend limited resources
(our tax dollars) on a product we all eventually need (medical care).
A study done by the Economic Council of Canada[3] found that even
though we all need more medical attention as we age, the overall
increase in health care expenditures is only 1 percent per capita per
year.[4] Those who are worried about the impending doom and collapse of the health care system are usually projecting ahead by thirty
to forty years. Given that time horizon, the accumulated health
costs can look overwhelming. But an economy can also counteract
by generating substantial increases in wealth to more than cover the
added strain of health expenditures. However, the days of unre-
strained medical costs may be behind us; provincial and federal governments are under increasing pressure to hold the line on them.
This will probably result in less high-cost hospital care and more
out-patient facilities. We'll be spending smarter, not more. As we get
older, we'll have to make tough choices about how to spend our
health care dollars but there's no evidence this will be any more of a
burden to future generations.[5]

That's not to suggest that we will be able to afford all the rich social programs we've come to expect over the last few decades. But the strains on these programs were evident long before the mass retirements expected over the next twenty years. Just because the population is aging and the work force is shrinking, Canadians do not necessarily have to expect a declining standard of living.

NOTES

[1] This drop in productivity has been a subject of considerable study, but Canada wasn't alone. Productivity rates dropped in most industrial countries including the United States, Japan, and West Germany. It doesn't take much to improve living standards. A modest 2 percent growth in productivity will lead to a seven-fold increase in real national income over a century.

[2] Low savings is the main reason poor countries remain poor. With low income levels, poor countries consume all they produce and more, leaving nothing in order to build their capital base and eliminating the foundation for future growth.

[3] See Jac-Andre Boulet and Gilles Grenier, *Health Expenditures in Canada and the Impact of Demographic Changes on Future Government Health Insurance Program Expenditures* (Economic Council of Canada, discussion paper 123, Ottawa, 1978).

[4] In another study, Canada's chief statistician arrived at roughly the same conclusion. In his study, "Can We Afford an Aging Population?" Ivan D. Fellegri said that, " ... should long-term economic growth continue as it has in the past and unit costs evolve as assumed, then public spending in health, education and pensions would represent 50 years from now about the same claim on the economy as present in spite of the aging of the population." See Ivan D. Fellegri, "Can We Afford an Aging Population?", *Canadian Economic Observer* (Ottawa: Statistics Canada, catalogue no. 11-010, October 1988), pp. 41–42.

[5] M.C. Wolfson, "International Perspectives on the Economics of Aging," *Canadian Economic Observer*, August 1991.

MYTH 13

THE GST IS A BAD TAX

N obody likes taxes. But of all taxes, perhaps the most universally despised and misunderstood is the goods and services tax (GST) that came into effect in January 1991. Consumers now pay taxes on services (as well as goods), something they have never had to do before. Consumers are reminded of this tax every time they make a purchase.

Critics of the GST have argued that the tax would fuel inflation, tax the poor more than the rich, cost the government millions to administer, and slow economic growth, to say nothing of the pain and anguish it would cause everyone while adjusting to it.[1] Despite arguments and evidence to the contrary, however, the myth still persists that the GST was a bad idea and the feeling still lingers that we would have been better off leaving things the way they were. What many forget is that things were not that "good" with the earlier federal sales tax, or Manufacturers' Sales Tax (MST), that the GST replaced. The GST is a broader tax rate applying to a wider range of products, replacing a tax that carried a higher rate but covered a narrower range of products.[2] The only advantage of the old tax was that we did not see it and assumed someone else paid for it. Even Albertans, who claim they have never had to pay a sales tax, had to pay the MST. The truth is that the MST was doing serious damage to the economy.

WHY THE GST AND WHY NOW?

The first thing to understand is what constitutes a good tax. To most people, a "good tax" is a contradiction in terms; but governments have to raise money somehow, so the question is, what's the best and fairest way to do it? On this question governments should follow two principles when considering raising taxes: the equity principle and the efficiency principle. The first has to do with making sure that the tax burden falls mainly on those who can afford to pay more; while the second simply means that the tax should leave the economy in the same condition it found it in, or do as little damage to the economy as possible.[3] In other words, a tax should not distort buying patterns, change our purchases from one product to another, or favour one good over another. For example, if the rate of taxes is higher for clothing than for movies, consumers will buy fewer clothes and see more movies, thus giving an artificial incentive to invest in services and away from goods production. For the economy to work efficiently, the decision about how society allocates its resources should be left to the consumer and not distorted by the tax system. On that basis the MST failed on both counts.

Just because the MST applied to manufactured goods, does not mean that manufacturers paid for it. Like most taxes they were passed along to the consumer without regard to questions of fairness, thus violating the equity principle. In the language of economics, the federal sales tax was a regressive tax, which means that the poor pay a higher proportion of their income than the rich.

The federal sales tax was also guilty of distorting consumption preferences, thereby violating the efficiency principle. The MST rate of 13.5 percent was applied to a narrow range of manufactured goods while services generally went untaxed. In effect it changed relative prices between goods and services making manufactured goods more expensive in relation to services. It is not surprising that consumers tended to buy more services. But bad as these things are, they probably would not have been enough to compel a government to commit political suicide by introducing an unpopular tax.

The real damage of the old federal sales tax was that it was slowly dragging the economy down by something economists call the deadweight loss of the tax. This means that the economy was becoming less efficient, and therefore less productive, as governments continued raising revenues with a system that was damaging to the economy (Figure 13.1). In other words, any tax discourages output by causing a fall in production.

One might wonder whether the gain in efficiency from lowering taxes on goods is not cancelled out by the deadweight loss from the new tax on services.[4] The simple answer is yes, but not by as much. The reason for this is that the deadweight loss arising from a tax increases more quickly in proportion to the scale of the tax

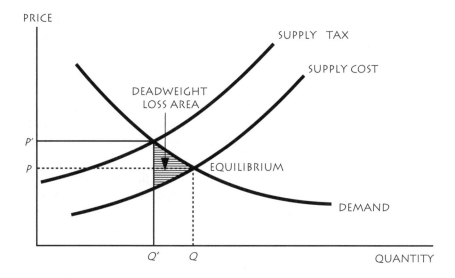

PRICE

SUPPLY TAX

SUPPLY COST

DEADWEIGHT
LOSS AREA

P'

P   EQUILIBRIUM

DEMAND

Q'   Q   QUANTITY

NOTE: A tax causes a leftward shift in the supply curve and a new price, quantity equilibrium from P, Q to P'Q'. At the new equilibrium consumers pay a higher price with less output. But there is also a "deadweight loss" represented by the triangle made up of a loss in 'consumer' (upper part of the triangle) and 'producer' surplus.

FIGURE 13.1   HOW TAXES CREATE DEADWEIGHT LOSS

itself. A broader but lower tax rate is more efficient by encouraging more production than a higher but narrower tax rate. Most economists estimate that the GST will have a smaller deadweight loss per dollar of revenue raised because its rate of taxation is lower than the MST.

These are not the only benefits of introducing the GST. One of the major challenges facing governments is to encourage more investment in order to improve productivity, competitiveness and employment. Instead of helping matters, the manufacturers' sales tax was discouraging investment because most investment goods are manufactured goods. The manufacturing sector was actually shrinking, in part because of the distortions caused by the former tax. Our antiquated tax system was unwittingly making Canada less competitive.[5] To make matters worse, the federal sales tax also tended to favour imports, taxed exports and was costly and complicated to administer.

This was nothing new. One commission or another has been recommending that we get rid of the MST since 1940. We have had to wait over fifty years for something to be done. It is estimated that by replacing the MST with the GST, the economy will add as much as $10 billion to the annual output. By lowering the tax on manufactured goods, the government has reduced the deadweight loss on the taxation of goods production. Politicians persisted with the old tax mainly because it was politically expedient. By 1991, the MST was bringing in over $18 billion a year. To compensate for the high taxes in manufacturing, the federal government implemented numerous tax write-offs and exemptions for businesses. By the end, the MST applied to only 75,000 firms, with over 22,000 special rules and exemptions. The real winners during the era of the manufacturers' sales tax were the army of tax lawyers and accountants hired to find tax loopholes.

Part of the reason that the tax was eventually changed has to do with an attempt to find a way to make our industries more competitive internationally. Other countries had already implemented or were moving towards a value added tax, such as the GST, that taxed consumption rather than production.[6] (The United States is the only major country that does not have some form of value-added tax.) With the free trade agreement with the United States, it was time to reduce the tax burden on the goods-producing sector of the economy.

THE PUBLIC'S REACTION TO THE GST

Although the reasons why the GST was introduced are valid, they still didn't impress the average Canadian. Questions were asked such as, "Won't the GST be inflationary?", "What's to keep the retailer from keeping prices the way they were and pocketing the differences?" and "Won't the tax affect the poor more than the rich?" The answer in each case is no. To find out why, each argument should be examined in turn.

First, one of the biggest fears about the new tax was that it would be inflationary. There was an increase in prices when the tax was introduced in January 1991, but that was a one-time increase. The consumer price index went up 2.4 percent for January. At that rate, inflation would have gone up about 30 percent for the year if it had continued but it didn't. Inflation for the year was 5.6 percent and only half of that was due to the GST. For inflation to exist, the rate of prices has to rise over an extended period of time. By mid 1992, the consumer price index was down to 1.1 percent, the lowest level in over thirty years. Clearly the GST wasn't inflationary. What did change, of course, was relative prices as the price of services went up and those of goods tended to go down with the removal of the MST.

The second major concern was that the supplier or retailer would not pass on the savings to the consumer from the elimination of the MST. But consider the following: many retailers selling appliances, for example, have two objectives, making money and keeping or increasing market share. If they had their costs reduced by 13.5 percent because of the removal of the MST, and then added a 7 percent GST, their prices should drop by 6.5 percent. If they did not pass on those savings to the consumer, it would not take long for competitors to get more business by lowering prices. Competition would guarantee that cost reductions would be passed along. In fact because of the recession, when the GST was introduced many retailers absorbed it outright. Even though the GST is essentially a tax on consumption, who pays the tax depends on the bargaining power between buyer and sellers.[7] Besides, if consumers are truly price insensitive, businesses do not have to wait around for tax reduction to raise prices if they want to make more money. Sellers always have the option to increase their prices if the market will bear it.

The third concern was that the poor would be affected more than the rich with a tax no one can avoid. In other words, the GST is regressive in breaking the principle of equity. It is true that government revenues are higher under the GST, but the government gives it right back in tax credits. Anyone making less than $35,000 annually gets a full refund. This takes care of most of the regressive nature of the tax. Even without the rebate, the GST is a fairer tax because it compels more people to pay their share of taxes and is more difficult to avoid.

However, the government did increase revenues more than expected. This happened mainly because a large part of the underground economy that had escaped taxation earlier was now caught in the tax net. (This is also what happened in New Zealand when they introduced their own version of the GST). Firms can only get a refund on the GST if they file for one. Once a firm files, they can not claim for credits on their purchases while avoiding taxes on their sales.

Finally, some have argued that the GST was simply too expensive to implement; that is, the benefits are not worth the cost. The Department of Finance has estimated that the start-up costs and administration of the tax were about $700 million for 1990. This probably underestimates the cost of getting the program off the ground as thousands of businesses spent time and money learning the new system. However, as we've already seen, the manufacturers' sales tax was also expensive to administer. When you consider the loss of economic efficiency created by the MST, the start-up costs of the GST seem like a bargain.

HAS THE GST DONE ITS JOB?

Now that we have some experience with the new value-added tax, we can ask if it has performed the way that it should and it seems, so far, it has. Consumer prices did jump when the tax was introduced, but continued to rise only moderately throughout 1991. On the other hand, prices for machinery, equipment and other investment goods went down. The bad news is, however, that spending in services and the retail sector has gone down as the cost of services went up in relation to manufactured goods. Both of these developments were anticipated with the new tax. On the negative side the federal government made the tax too complicated, which resulted in massive foul-ups and errors by first time filers. In hindsight the government should have avoided exceptions to the tax, which it made in response to lobbying by special interest groups.[8] It would have been better to reduce the overall rate allowing no or fewer exemptions. Another glaring error was the refusal of the provinces to blend their sales taxes into the GST, thereby making tax collection more difficult than it need be.

Overall, the GST, even with all the start-up problems, is a better tax than the one it replaced. If taxes are to be paid it is better that they are obvious rather than hidden. With the declining competitiveness of the country fuelled by the MST, it is better to try to levy a tax that is fairer and more likely to increase production.

NOTES

1. Even cross-border shopping has been blamed on the GST, although the real factor pushing Canadians to shop in the border states has more to do with the exchange rate than taxes.

2. There are some exceptions. The GST does not apply to some groceries, agricultural and fish products, prescription drugs and medical devices, track betting, day-care services, financial and educational services, and long-term rents.

3. Unfortunately taxes that are most efficient are often the least equitable. To get more efficiency, more equity has to be sacrificed.

4. The extent of the deadweight loss depends on the elasticity of demand of the goods that are being taxed. The more elastic the demand curve is, the higher the deadweight loss. That's one reason governments tend to tax inelastic products, such as tobacco and alcohol, more than elastic products, such as fruit juice and toys.

5. In 1989 the Economic Council estimated that despite tax credits to offset taxes on manufactured goods, the average tax on investment was still about 4 percent. See William Watson and Andrew Coyne, "Special Report: The GST," *The Financial Post*, 19 December 1989, p. 29.

6. The GST, like any value-added tax, is based on taxing consumption rather than production. But that doesn't mean that consumers always pay the tax. Suppliers are charged a set tax, in the case of the GST 7 percent, for the added value to production. Production costs along with the tax are passed through to the next purchaser. Each purchaser is entitled to get a refund on the GST charged by their supplier.

7. Even a monopolist would lower prices with a tax cut if it wanted to maximize profits. A lower tax means a lower marginal cost, and profits are maximized where marginal cost equals marginal revenue (MC = MR).

8. Groceries are exempted on the grounds that the poor spend a higher portion of their income on food than the rich. Even racetrack betting is exempted from the GST. Questions of equity are best handled through credits and refunds rather than tax exemptions.

MYTH 14
HIGHER TAXES MEAN LESS WORK (AND VICE-VERSA)

I n 1981, the Reagan administration conducted one of the biggest social and economic experiments in modern times.[1] It was based on the simple notion that people hate taxes, and if they were cut, people would work harder because they could keep more of what they earned. If people earn more, they in turn would save more, invest more and start more businesses to the advantage of the entire economy. This supply side economics came to be popularly known as "Reaganomics." The logic of the theory was impeccable. Supply siders maintained that the higher the marginal tax rate, the lower the amount of effort put out by workers. The result was, therefore, obvious: if the government wanted people to work harder, all it had to do was lower taxes.

From there it is a short step to conclude that if people work harder governments would benefit with higher revenues. Everyone wins: the taxpayer with lower taxes, governments with richer coffers, and the economy in general with a fiscal shot in the arm. The Reagan advisers predicted that with lower taxes the government would be able to balance its budget by 1983 and still spend billions to build up its military. What could be more sensible and straightforward? There was only one problem— it didn't work.

Government revenues collapsed drastically causing the U.S. national debt to double. What happened? How could such logic and common sense have failed so miserably? The Reagan government discovered what most theoreticians have known for a long time— what looks good on paper does not always turn out in practice. Workers when offered higher wages might work harder, but not always and not under all conditions.

INCOME VS. SUBSTITUTION EFFECT

To understand why Reaganomics did not work, we have to look at the choices or trade-offs between labour and leisure. Think of leisure as any other good in that it produces what economists call positive utility. Given that each day has a fixed number of hours, we can only increase our leisure time by working fewer hours. To get more leisure, we give up more work. There's an implicit trade-off between work and play. When we have a trade-off between these two goods, the opportunity cost of leisure time is measured in lost wages or money income. Put another way, the opportunity cost of leisure is the sacrificed goods and services that extra money income can buy. If a net wage is $15 an hour, an extra hour of leisure will cost $15, or the things $15 can buy. Taxes decrease the opportunity cost of leisure. The higher the tax, the less expensive it becomes to substitute leisure for work, and this is known as the substitution effect.

A proportional tax rate reduces the opportunity cost of labour by an equal amount. For example, if a worker is making $15 an hour, a 33 percent tax rate will reduce the after-tax on labour income to $10. A progressive tax rate takes a bigger and bigger bite out of labour income, which reduces the opportunity cost of leisure time even more. Both proportional and progressive taxes reduce the opportunity cost of leisure but by different amounts depending on the hours worked.

The implications for tax policy seem straightforward. When taxes go up, people will work less because leisure time becomes less expensive. If that is true, it should also hold that a reduction in taxes, whether proportional or progressive, will encourage more work as people substitute work for leisure. This is because the opportunity cost of leisure goes up. Arthur Laffer, one of Reagan's advisers, concluded that tax cuts would actually increase government revenues as more workers chose to work and earn more. The relationship between government revenues and taxes was captured in what came to be known as the Laffer Curve (see Figure 14.1). However, Laffer overlooked another effect going on at the same time: the income effect.

It is true that as wages go up, or taxes fall, more labour is offered, but there is a limit and that is when the income effect starts

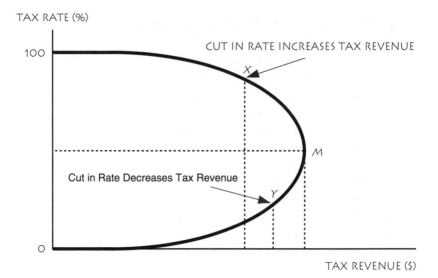

TAX RATE (%)

100 CUT IN RATE INCREASES TAX REVENUE

X

M

Cut in Rate Decreases Tax Revenue

Y

O

TAX REVENUE ($)

NOTE: If the tax rate is at *X*, reducing taxes will increase tax revenues to the point at *M*. If the tax rate is at *Y*, a tax increase will bring in more revenues. The optimal tax rate is at *M*.

FIGURE 14.1 THE LAFFER CURVE

to occur. As people earn more income, they feel richer and their demand for all goods and services goes up, including the demand for more leisure time. Just because someone receives more money does not mean that they will put in more hours of work. There comes a point when the income effect overrides the substitution effect and less labour is supplied as income increases. In this case if marginal tax rates are decreased more and more, this will eventually cause workers to put in fewer hours rather than more, contrary to what supply side theory tells us. American companies found this out when they started large-scale developments in Algeria after that country's independence from France was gained in 1962.[2] Algerian wages then were only about one-tenth those in the United States. To encourage more work, the U.S. companies paid Algerian workers one-third of the U.S. wage rates or three to four times the average wage in Algeria. Supply side economics would have predicted that higher wages would encourage more work; however, the opposite happened because workers could now afford to buy larger amounts of leisure time. (It is actually possible that people will work *more* in cases where taxes are raised as people try to maintain their previous standard of living.) These results are not unique to Third World

MYTH 14 — HIGHER TAXES MEAN LESS WORK (AND VICE-VERSA)

countries. It has been shown that people do not respond to changes in after-tax pay rates. There is actually a tendency for work effort to decline slightly. Many people have an optimum level of income, and higher after-tax pay reduces the number of hours needed to earn that income.

It is not enough to know what people might or might not do under certain conditions—we need to know "how much less" or "more" they will work. The question is essentially quantitative and not subject to logic alone. If taxes are cut by 25 percent, tax revenues will go down by the same amount if nobody works any harder. It has been estimated for the United States that for those in the lower tax rate category to pay the same amount of taxes, they would have to increase their work effort by two-and-one-half times the percentage increase in after-tax wage rates itself. In other words, for governments to replenish tax revenues from a tax cut, it takes an extraordinary amount of work effort.[3] Supply side advocates underestimated exactly how much work that would be. Besides, how people change their work effort in response to changes in wages depends on their occupation, age, sex, and a whole range of other factors that are difficult to measure.

POVERTY AND LESSONS FROM SUPPLY SIDE ECONOMICS

What does this mean for Canada? We can apply some of the lessons learned from the supply side economics experiment to the idea of introducing a negative income tax, or a guaranteed annual income in order to eliminate poverty and bring efficiency and equity to the tax structure without at the same time destroying the incentive to work. At one point or another, all of the three major political parties have endorsed an overhauling of the way we help the poor by supporting some system of negative income tax. The Macdonald Commission in 1985 proposed revamping the social security system in favour of a Universal Income Security Program. A guaranteed minimum income based on a negative income tax plan has been around for years.

Theoretically, the negative income tax plan is structured on certain ideas. It is thought that instead of having an inefficient system of welfare and income support programs to help the poor, we should replace the existing system by giving the poor a minimum income and, therefore, getting rid of poverty once and for all. It has been estimated that it would cost no more than 2 percent of GDP to bring poor families up to the poverty line and a decent standard of living. A negative income tax works as follows: If a family earns no income, they would get a "negative income" or grant of, say, $5,000. If that same family brings in $1,000 in income, this family would get a negative income of $4,500. If they were not allowed to keep more of their income, there would be no incentive to work for that extra income. A family earning $5,000 would receive $2,500 from the government, bringing their total income to $7,500. In other words, people below some break-even point (for example, $10,000) would be allowed to keep half of what they earn. After $10,000, workers would pay "positive taxes" on their income. Simply giving low-income families, or individuals, a lump sum to bring them up to the poverty line would wipe out any incentive to work. If everyone is guaranteed $10,000 if they don't work, why would anyone bother to earn anything below that amount? The working poor would be better off quitting their jobs.

The purpose behind the negative tax scheme is to eradicate poverty without destroying the incentive to work. That is the theory, but how does it work in practice? As with most economic and social questions, the answers are not so clear or obvious. The results of studies in the United States are disappointing. Negative income tax ended up making people work less. In some cases the disincentive to work increased almost 60 percent.[4]

In Canada in the mid 1970s, the federal government paid $17 million to over 1,000 families in Manitoba to test the idea of a negative income tax and its effects on work incentives. The program was called The Manitoba Basic Annual Income Experiment, or Mincome for short, and took about twenty years to complete. The findings from Mincome are not as discouraging as those in the United States. There is still a tendency for people to choose more leisure than earn more income, but its impact is small.[5] Negative income taxes do not discourage work as much as some might imagine, but they do not seem to encourage work either; however, there are advantages. A negative income tax is less costly to administer and is certainly fairer than the system we now have to transfer income to the poor. Those collecting welfare face a marginal tax rate of 100 percent if they earn any money outside the system—nothing destroys work effort more than that.

So who is right? That question is hard to answer. The Mincome experiment measured only the behaviour of those on the receiving end. What about the behaviour of those on the giving end who have to pay for the program with their taxes? In 1989 all three levels of government transferred $75.9 billion in cash payments under various income security programs in Canada.[6] Those transfers are growing faster than the growth in the economy. In 1989 that figure represented 11.6 percent of Canada's GDP compared to 8.5 percent in 1971. Of those funds only 21 percent went to the poor.[7] We know that lowering the tax rate will not necessarily increase the desire for more work even though leisure time becomes more expensive as its opportunity cost goes up. How then will people react to higher marginal tax rates and lower take home pay? For starters, some people will simply work less while others find ways of averting taxes with tax shelters. One of the easiest ways to avoid taxes is by taking more time off. If taxes really start climbing, more people join the "underground" economy and avoid paying taxes altogether. In the end this means lower wealth for society as a whole.

Helping the poor has always been a priority of Canada's governments. We've done a better job than our neighbours to the south in this respect. Economists and politicians too often see poverty as an income problem, so when we try to give the poor more money by whatever means, we find it is an expensive proposition, and one that turns out to have implications for those who receive as well as those who give. But changing the tax system simply on a hunch, without a complete investigation of how workers and taxpayers react to tax changes can have drastic consequences for government revenues as it did in the United States. The principles are the same on the welfare side. It is not enough to give the poor more income without first understanding how people's incentives to work are affected by how they receive the money in the first place.

NOTES

[1]   This was know as the Roth–Kemp tax plan, which reduced income taxes by 25 percent.

[2]   Roger LeRoy Miller, Daniel K. Benjamin and Douglas C. North, *The Economics of Public Issues*, 8th ed. (New York: Harper Collins, 1990), p. 129.

[3]   Most people who could work already had jobs and with very little opportunity to increase their hours of work even if they wanted. The problem of encouraging more work effort from an aging population may even be harder as older workers and those approaching retirement begin to value their leisure time more. See Benjamin Friedman, *Day of Reckoning* (New York: Vintage Books, 1989), p. 242.

[4]   These results come from studies done in Seattle and Denver by Michael Keely and Philip Robbins, discussed in their articles "Labour Supply Effects and Costs of Alternative Negative Income Tax Programs," *Journal of Human Resources*, winter 1978.

[5]   Derek Hum and Wayne Simpson for the Economic Council of Canada, *Income Maintenance, Work Effort, and the Canadian Mincome Experiment* (Ottawa: Supply and Services 1991), p. XVI.

[6]   Raj K. Chawla, "Dependence on government transfer payment, 1971–1989," in *Perspectives on Labour and Income*, StatsCan, summer 1991.

[7]   One U.S. study found that the government had to spend $350 to get $100 to the poor. The rest was simply wasted getting the $100 to the poor, and provided a massive efficiency loss to society. If we don't think the same thing happens in Canada, consider job-training programs, which are geared to helping the working poor upgrade their skills and get better paying jobs. From 1976 to 1990, the federal government spent over $12 billion on these programs. The apprenticeship programs have been a dismal failure. There's a 40 percent drop out rate, and of those that finish, their chances of higher wages or of getting a job are no better than those who drop out. Society suffers a double failure: our skills aren't any better, and the $12 billion is lost forever. See Ernest B. Akyeampong, "Apprentices: Graduate and dropout Labour market performances," StatsCan, *Perspectives on Labour and Income*, spring 1991.

THE NATIONAL DEBT IS A BURDEN ON OUR GRANDCHILDREN

In the spring of 1991, the former Minister of Finance, Michael Wilson, appeared on stage with a small boy in a campaign to fight the national debt. The small boy had come to contribute his allowance towards the nation's financial problems. In the background a monitor flashed how the government was going into debt at the rate of $3 million an hour and told how, on a per capita basis, the debt was about $15,500 for every man, woman, and child.

This scene was symbolic of how Canada's growing debt had come to be seen as an inevitable burden on younger generations and the feeling that if something wasn't done to eradicate the country's debt and deficit, the problem would only get worse. The scene was both poignant and cynical: poignant because it drew attention to Canada's mounting debt; cynical because it was used as a "photo opportunity" for the minister (who must have known that the solution is much more complicated than just having people donate to pay off the debt).

Conventional thought about the national debt and deficit is that unless we buckle down and pay them off, they will remain as millstones around the neck of future generations who will curse us to our graves for accumulating such monstrous debts. But is the national debt a true burden on our grandchildren? To understand the answer let's examine how the debt came to be so big, how to think about it, and what its real consequences are.

THE NATIONAL DEBT: "MY, HOW YOU'VE GROWN!"

Let's take a brief look at how the debt got so big. In the mid 1970s, the federal government reformed unemployment insurance, welfare and pension plans by indexing them to the level of inflation. As prices went up, spending on these programs rose automatically (practically guaranteeing future inflation); and as these programs grew, so did government spending. The same decade also saw world oil prices rise dramatically. The government, in order to protect the provinces from increased energy costs, cut energy taxes and increased subsidies to the more energy-deficient provinces through the National Energy Program. The higher energy costs, along with imported inflation from the United States, led to higher prices pushing the inflation rates into the low 'teens. The government decided to fight higher prices by "cooling off" the economy with high interest rates.

The good times were over, and the suffering began. The higher interest rates created lower demand for goods and services resulting eventually in lower prices. Personal and business bankruptcies soared and the unemployment rate was over 13 percent by 1983. Interest rates were over 20 percent. The recession, which was caused by fighting inflation, was the most severe since the depression of the 1930s. As the recession set in, government transfer payments to provinces (mainly unemployment insurance) escalated uncomfortably. Since of course, recessions also mean that less is collected in taxes the government had to borrow money to meet the higher transfer payments by selling bonds. As the recession dragged on, the fastest growing part of government spending was interest payments on the growing debt.

Even though the economy began to recover after 1983, the government was never able to pay off the interest share of federal spending. Government finances have been in deficit every year since 1975. By 1991, the interest paid on servicing the national debt made up 28 percent of total spending by the government, or about $43 billion annually out of a total budget of $151 billion. Compare that to 11 percent in the mid 1970s. Every time the interest rate goes up 1 percent, the national debt rises about $4 billion annually. It is little wonder that the government hasn't been able to harness the deficit despite cut-backs.[1]

Although federal spending continued to climb in the 1980s, revenues, as a share of Gross Domestic Product (GDP), went down. This was caused mainly by greater tax transfers to the provinces, income tax cuts in the 1970s, and slower than expected economic growth after 1975.[2] Tax revenues dropped from 19.8 percent (as a share of GDP) in 1975 to 17.4 percent by 1986. The growing government deficit was caused mainly by lower than expected revenues from taxation, and unprecedented debt servicing charges. The irony is that the deficit explosion was the unexpected, as well as unwelcome, result of the government's anti-inflation policy of the early 1980s. The larger its interest obligations, the more the federal government had to borrow in the face of disappointing tax revenues. Now trapped in a vicious circle, in trying to solve the problem of high prices with high interest rates, the government had saddled the country with a new and more intractable problem — a growing debt that will not go away anytime soon.

HOW TO THINK ABOUT THE DEBT AND DEFICIT

Now that we have a rough outline of what caused the problem, let's look at how big the debt and deficits really are. It's important to know how to think about the dimensions of the problem before scrambling off to try to solve it. To begin with, most people are overwhelmed by the sheer dimensions of the debt. In 1991, the debt stood at approximately $420 billion. Measured in raw terms, the debt is big. There's no question about that.

However, if we look at the deficit from another point of view we can more accurately examine its real dimensions. To begin, the deficit is only one year's shortfall between what the government spends and takes in taxes. You could say that the total Canadian debt is the accumulated deficits since Confederation. The nominal deficit is the actual deficit *unadjusted* for inflation. If we want to know the real deficit, we have to remove the effects of inflation. For example, if prices go up 10 percent this year, and the deficit goes up 9 percent, then the "real" value of the deficit actually drops by 1 percent. In 1989, the nominal deficit was more than 3 percent of GDP, but the real deficit was less than 2 percent. In 1981 the federal government actually ran a small surplus even though the nominal deficit was positive.

Economists also look at it in another way: as a share of the size of the overall economy, or gross domestic product. In these terms, the federal debt is around 60 percent of national income. That's a substantial increase from 1975 when it was 37 percent. But we've been there before. Over 100 percent when Canada was carrying the large debts from the Great Depression and the Second World War (see Figure 15.1). It's not so much the actual size of the debt in terms of dollars that's important, but its size in relation to the whole economy for any given year. It's the same as putting a mortgage on a house. A $400,000 mortgage is large when the value of the house is $500,000, but it looks more manageable when the house appreciates to $1 million. As the value of the nation's assets grows, the relative size of the national debt shrinks. It is the *relative* size of the debt that counts, not the actual size. But even this analogy doesn't take into consideration Canada's true assets. Who can put a value on the mines, resources, factories, and land, along with the skills and knowledge of the entire population? Whatever it is, it would certainly dwarf the size of the national debt many times over. To paraphrase the economist Robert Heilbroner and Peter Bernstein,[3] it would be a fortunate bank indeed that held the mortgage on the Canadian economy for a mere $420 billion.

The next question, of course, is whether we can afford to service the debt or keep up the interest payments. It's important to understand that the actual burden of the public debt is the share of income it takes to carry it; in other words, what percent of national income goes to paying the interest on the debt. Since 1985, although

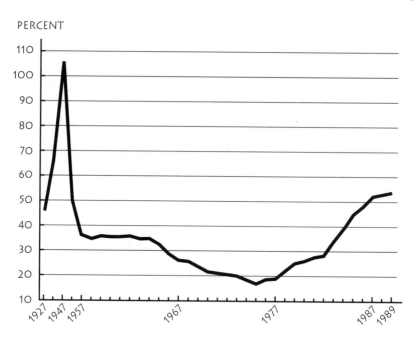

PERCENT

Source: Department of Finance Budget Papers (20 February 1990).

FIGURE 15.1   NATIONAL DEBT AS A PERCENTAGE OF GDP

MYTH 15 — THE NATIONAL DEBT IS A BURDEN ON OUR GRANDCHILDREN

the national debt has increased, our capacity to service it has also improved because our income has grown. In fact, then, Canada is nowhere near not being able to afford to carry the interest on its debt.[4]

DOESN'T THE NATIONAL DEBT LEAD TO BAD THINGS?

The debt and deficit may be smaller than we think when we measure the true assets in Canada and take inflation into consideration, but that doesn't address the anxiety of most people who still think the deficit is too big. Besides, some argue, the deficit causes a whole stream of other problems, such as forcing up interest rates and pushing up inflation.

Some argue that deficits put pressure on interest rates. The argument is that there's only so much public and private savings out there, and if governments run high deficits they compete with the private sector for these funds. The higher the demand, the higher the interest rates to attract the needed funding. Economists call this the crowding out effect. Looked at in another way, the more the government uses up of total national savings, the less there is available for the private sector. It sounds plausible in theory, but there's not much evidence to back it up. One theory holds that it doesn't matter whether the government pays for the deficit through current taxes or borrows by selling bonds. Debt financing or paying for government spending with taxes are equivalent. The main reason is that people know that deficit financing means more taxes down the road, so they consume less and save today to adjust for higher taxes tomorrow. Higher savings mean more money for the capital markets and lower real interest rates as well. The implication is that the size of the deficit doesn't really matter! Odd as this theory may be, there's evidence to support that it may be true.[5]

There are those who argue that inflation is a consequence of high deficits. But that depends on how the government finances the deficit. Here, it has three options: raising taxes, selling bonds to the Bank of Canada (i.e. printing money), or borrowing from the public by selling bonds. The Canadian government uses this last option mainly because the other two carry more consequences for the economy. If the government paid the debt with higher taxes, there would probably be more unemployment because of lower overall demand for goods and services. If it printed more money to pay its debts, the increase in the supply of money would probably result in more inflation. That's why the government borrows to pay its debts, because in the short run it doesn't destroy jobs or increase prices.[6]

OUR GRANDCHILDREN BOTH GAIN AND LOSE FROM A DEFICIT

The government's borrowing of the difference each year to make up for its financial shortfalls, does not come without costs. After all, the government has to pay interest on the debt it accumulates. Many people have the impression that unless this debt is paid off, there will come a day of reckoning when all the bills will come due. They feel that we should pay off the debt and keep the interest instead of wasting it. That sounds plausible, but there's a flaw. Those who pay the taxes also get the interest from those government bonds. This includes all the people, businesses and pension plans that own government securities. The interest paid on the debt doesn't go into some black hole forever. If we ever repaid the debt, the generation that paid it off would also get the proceeds. It might be a burden to some, but others benefit. This is another way of saying we owe it to ourselves.[7]

It's true that debts incurred helping the present generations of taxpayers will have to be paid by taxing future generations. If the government decides to enrich the nation's social security fund with deficit financing, those not yet born will pay higher taxes throughout their high-income earning years, but eventually will benefit in their retirement years (when their incomes decline) because of the very programs their taxes have supported. When President Reagan cut taxes in the early 1980s, it was estimated that a thirty-year-old taxpayer would save $12,000 (U.S.) over his or her lifetime. Yet that individual would receive from $10,000 to $15,000 less in today's dollars because retirement benefits were decreased partially to pay for the tax decrease. What seemed like the lifting of a huge burden created a small effect overall.[8] Our children and grandchildren will inherit not only higher taxes, but also the vast richness of this country, including the accumulated knowledge and technology, and fixed capital of past generations—the very things needed to increase future incomes in their lifetimes. Much of those assets are the results of debts incurred by the government today.

However, an uncontrolled and growing national debt can do the economy harm. The main problem with our growing debt is that the discretionary part of the budget is growing slower than the nondiscretionary part. This means that the government is allocating a larger share of tax revenues in areas it has little or no control over such as servicing the debt, which put at risk some of our social programs such as health, education, social services and equalization programs. These funds could have been used to build the nation's capital stock and infrastructure as a foundation on which to increase future per capita income. The more we spend in areas where governments have little control, the less is available for highways, water and sewage systems, and government research and development. Private investment will be discouraged if governments can't increase their spending on fixed capital formation. This is the real cost to future generations: we'll have a smaller capital base and a less-developed infrastructure on which to increase our overall standard of living.[9]

Should we be concerned about the national debt? Yes, but not for the reasons that most people believe. The important point is not to take drastic steps to pay it off, but rather to manage its growth. A government is not constrained to balance its budget year after year like a household or a business. Cutting the deficit too quickly would create more problems than it solves.

NOTES

[1] Government spending (mainly unemployment insurance and welfare) also increased during the recession of 1981. But social programs as a whole held steady as a share of GDP throughout the 1980s.

[2] In 1977 Ottawa introduced the Established Program Financing Act, which transferred health care and post-secondary education funds to the provinces. In 1989 this amounted to $8.6 billion, or 7.9 percent of all federal revenues.

[3] Robert Heilbroner and Peter Bernstein, *The Debt and the Deficit: False Alarms/Real Possibilities* (New York: W.W. Norton and Company, 1989), p. 37.

[4] The federal government deficit declined as a share of GDP from 6.7 percent in 1984-85, to 3.7 percent in 1990-1991, lower than the U.S. share. Source: *The Federal Budget*, 25 February, 1992, p. 115.

5   This theory, called Ricardian Equivalence after the seventeenth-century British economist David Ricardo, has come back into vogue after being revived by Robert Barro at Harvard University.

6   Some economists argue that even if the government borrows, the results are inflationary. They reason that as the deficit increases, the political temptation to solve the problem by printing money will be too great. The government is simply putting off inevitable inflation by borrowing in the present. So far, there's little to support that case. Even Conservative economist Robert E. Lucas Jr., at the University of Chicago, no longer believes deficits are inflationary. See Michael Parkin and Robin Bade, *Economics* (Don Mills: Addison-Wesley, 1991), p. 799.

7   Critics argue that this line of reasoning is not valid because some of the debt is held by Japanese and German investors. This is true, but 75 percent of the debt is still financed at home. Besides, by borrowing from foreigners, we are able to invest in the Canadian economy at higher levels than if we were to depend solely on domestic savings.

8   Lawrence J. Fotlikoff, "Deficit Thinking," *The Sciences*, May/June, 1989.

9   As nondiscretionary spending goes up as a share of total government spending, more pressure will be put on cutting back on our social programs. In 1991, the federal government won an important battle with the provinces in the supreme court ruling that said that Ottawa wasn't obligated to make equalization payments to the provinces for certain programs. The battle over the continuation of social spending is just beginning in this country.

MYTH 16

ONLY BUSINESSES CREATE, WHILE ONLY GOVERNMENTS WASTE

overnment policies regarding rent control, pay equity and minimum wages can end up making things worse rather than better. However, aside from these more obvious programs, there are many other examples of public sector failures and incompetence. In the past decade alone governments have lost billions of dollars propping up weak industries and supporting ill-conceived projects. One has only to think of the $1 billion lost by offshore oil drilling at Hibernia; the $1.4 billion federal write-off of the Canadair *Challenger* aircraft; the millions of dollars lost supporting defunct technologies; Mirabel airport outside Montreal; and the support of unprofitable steel mills in Eastern Canada. In the 1980s the federal government's misguided program to encourage R&D through research and tax credits cost the country untold millions through fraud and corruption.

These are the projects we hear about every day in the media. Furthermore, there are the less obvious (but expensive) things, such as royal commission reports that collect dust once finished; bureaucratic redundancies; and inefficient regulations and programs.

It is not surprising that the 1980s were a difficult time for governments. The last decade was renowned for cries to get the public sector out of the way of business so that business could get on with the job of creating wealth. Government was too prevalent and needed to be reduced in influence through deregulation and greater privatization of the economy. The growing perception was that governments do not create wealth, they just redistribute it (at best), and waste it (at worst).

However, it is not always the case that governments only waste, while businesses create. Here we have to deal with two myths: first, that a dollar spent by governments is less productive than a dollar spent in the private sector; and second, that the private sector is less wasteful of society's scarce resources.

IN DEFENCE OF MORE CAPITAL SPENDING

Despite the shortcomings of government's role in the market economy, not all tax dollars or government spending have the same impacts on the economy. Governments do a good job when it comes to providing services, such as education and health services, or public goods, such as street lights. Without governments, there is no guarantee that these things would be available to everyone. Generally speaking, government spending at the federal, provincial, and municipal levels, can be classified into three broad areas: consumption, which includes everything from paper clips to education and health care; transfers to individuals and business including pensions, welfare, UI payments, and industrial incentives to companies; and lastly, fixed capital formation, a term which encompasses sewers, bridges, highways, public transit, etc. It is the last category that we are concerned with. Investment in this last sector has been slower than transfers to individuals. The less public capital spending there is, the less the private sector spends as well.[1]

The myth that private spending is independent of public spending is at the heart of this misunderstanding. The private sector can only function well if the public sector provides the necessary roads, transportation networks and infrastructure. If bridges, highways and public transport facilities are allowed to run down for lack of spending and maintenance, then that directly affects the performance of private investment and the overall economy.

Aside from those wealthy enough to use private means of transportation, the majority of us have to rely on buses, subways, and public highways to add value to the system. In this sense, the private and public networks are inextricably linked. Even the new terminal at Pearson International Airport in Toronto is both a public and private facility. Still, provincial and municipal governments have allowed their share of investment in capital formation to fall to only 10 percent of private capital formation, the lowest level in forty years.[2] There is a growing body of evidence that the neglect and underinvestment in our roads, highway, transit, and water and sewage treatment facilities has started to affect the performance of the economy and is a major reason for the decline in productivity over the last two decades. In the United States, one study found that the decline in public capital stock was the most powerful explanation for America's productivity decline over the past fifteen years.[3] When capital formation was high in the 1950s and 1960s, labour productivity averaged 4.5 percent. As infrastructure investment began to decline in Canada in the 1970s and 1980s, productivity came down with it to approximately 1.5 percent per year. At a rate of 2.5 percent per year, we can expect real wages and the standard of living to double every twenty-eight years. At the current rate we have to wait forty-eight years.

The problem is that to bring the nation's infrastructure up to par is expensive. The cost of bringing Canada's highways up to minimum standards is estimated to be almost $13 billion. Over 22 percent of the country's 3,434 bridges will need major work over the next five years and the longer we wait to do the repairs the more expensive they become. It's understandable how this type of situation comes about: politicians spend money where the political needs are greatest (such as social programs) particularly during recessions and economic downturns. A bridge that needs fixing or a sewage treatment plant needing repair waits until the next year. But the neglect cannot go on forever. Sooner or later a crumbling highway or a crowded airport will affect production and economic efficiency. Whether the government wants to take money away from other programs is up to politicians to decide. What is clear is that underinvesting in public fixed capital stock will have negative effects on our standard of living in the future.

It is important to understand that the way in which governments spend is almost as important as what they spend on. Therefore, one way to increase public sector efficiency is for public officials to be more scrupulous about how they spend our tax dollars. Evidence in the United States shows that when government bureaucracies are decentralized and open to outside competition, they can become more efficient. In Phoenix, for example, garbage collection was awarded to a private company in competition with the Public Works Department. Six years later, Public Works won back the job after streamlining its operation, at a saving to the community. The same thing occurred in Chicago when the city's road maintenance department began competing successfully against private paving companies when tenders were open to competition.[4]

BUSINESSES WASTE RESOURCES, TOO

Coupled with the general myth that only governments waste resources is the notion that businesses always conserve them. The truth is, the private sector can be just as wasteful as governments — and in some cases even more so. Conventional thought is that privately held businesses cannot lose money indefinitely because they have to answer to shareholders, who expect to make a profit on their investment. Further, it is thought that if businesses continue to make mistakes they will suffer by losing money or going under and that, in the end, the market disciplines private business. On the other hand, we are used to viewing governments as having a different agenda in which making the highest return on investment is not necessarily a priority. However, it is important for us to see that if we start with the premise that we have limited resources available for our use, it makes little difference which sector wastes them. When mistakes in planning are made by GM or IBM and billions of dollars are lost, everyone suffers because society in general has fewer resources at its disposal. Thus, although a business may lose by going bankrupt, we are all losers just the same as when tax dollars are squandered.

In Canadian business history there are plenty of examples of gross waste in the private sector. In cases such as Dome petroleum where over $1 billion was lost, one can argue that shareholders were the big losers. But that's not the case with the bailout of Algoma by the Ontario government, which had to pour in $110 million in loan guarantees to salvage a bad deal by Dofasco. Governments had to come to the aid of depositors at great expense to the taxpayer when institutions such as Standard Trust, Principal and other trust companies failed. Chrysler and Massey-Ferguson also received massive government aid when they fell into trouble. A more recent example is the overdevelopment of commercial real estate, mainly in southern Ontario and Toronto as billions of dollars in equity was lost through overbuilding and financial miscalculation. Even the mighty Olympia & York, who were once considered invincible giants in real estate, had to seek bankruptcy protection. When markets fail on this scale, thousands of jobs are at risk and governments are forced, or blackmailed, into bailing out these companies.[5] Luckily for Canadian taxpayers, the federal and Ontario governments decided against providing loan guarantees for Olympia & York's multibillion dollar debt as their worldwide real estate holdings began unravelling.

Even when banks make poor investment decisions and lose money, such as the hundreds of millions of dollars that were lost through poor real estate investment, someone has to make up for it;

it usually ends up being the shareholder or client through devalued stock holdings or higher service charges. In the end we're all poorer because of those decisions.[6]

THE RISE OF PAPER ENTREPRENEURS

For more proof that the private sector can be wasteful, there are the new robber barons of the last decade who have made unimaginable fortunes almost overnight by questionable deal making, including the sale of junk bonds, leveraged buyouts and corporate raids, to name only a few of the new tactics. The U.S. firm, Kohlberg Kravis Roberts and Company, who engineered the Campeau fiasco (Robert Campeau, who lost billions of dollars in real estate and retail store takeovers in the United States, mainly by issuing high yield "junk bonds"), made $100 million on that deal alone and countless other millions by rearranging the ownership of existing firms with leveraged buyouts and by shifting financing away from equity and toward debt. This was justified on the grounds that firms could be made more efficient through mergers and acquisitions, although there seems to be little evidence that the economy is any more productive than before the takeover of the 1980s. In the end these paper entrepreneurs — lawyers, accountants, MBAs, and stockbrokers — became enormously rich, not by increasing the efficiency of existing companies but by redistributing wealth away from the workers and original bondholders.[7] In the end, the 1980s were a decade where some of the brightest minds on Bay Street and Wall Street were not used in the pursuit of creating wealth, but were wasted in the rigging of financial markets through arbitrage, a term to describe the calculation of which companies are most likely to become takeover candidates, and then betting heavily on the outcome.

This does not mean that governments should necessarily jump in to regulate all markets because the private sector is wasteful. The private sector still does a better job of creating wealth, while governments are better at issues of fairness. But those who advocate that business is always superior to the public sector in creating wealth are wrong.

NOTES

1   Irene Ip, *Big Spenders* (Toronto: C.D. Howe Institute, 1991), p. 61.

2   Ip, *Big Spenders*, p. 63.

3   David Alan Aschauer, "Is Public Expenditure Productive?", *Journal of Monetary Economics*, March 1989, pp. 177–200. Although the problem is bad enough in Canada, it is nothing compared with the degrading condition of the capital infrastructure in the United States where the Department of Transportation estimates that it would take a colossal $315 billion U.S. just to repair the nation's highways. The problem in the United States stems from the lowering of taxes on the rich with the Reagan administration, which was designed to encourage investment but ended up promoting private consumer spending instead and a drastic decline in public investment. Robert Reich of Harvard blames this for the rift between the symbolic analysts, or the rich, and their abrogation of responsibilities to the poor. See Robert. B. Riech, *The Work of Nations* (New York: Vintage, 1992).

4   David Osborne, "Government Means Business," *New York Times Magazine* (1 March 1992), p. 20. Studies in the United States show that the private sector can deliver a number of services, such as fire fighting, municipal transit, utility billing and tax assessment. One study found that towns with a population over 50,000 can have their garbage collected 30 percent cheaper when they hire private firms. See Steven E. Rhoads, "The Economist's View of the World," *Governments, Markets, and Public Policy* (Cambridge, England: Cambridge University Press, 1985), pp. 69–70.

5   Society often doesn't realize that any government program that protects companies from competition (such as industrial grants and subsidies, low interest loans, tariffs, import quota restrictions, procurement programs, and marketing boards that restrict dairy products imports) also wastes resources by indirectly discouraging efficient production.

6   An empty office is not a complete waste even if the company that owns it goes bankrupt. That building does not simply disappear. Assets change hands. But in the meantime those resources could have been used to earn a higher return in some other area. The loss to society is the difference in the rate of return for these investments.

7   For a brief introduction to the subject, see Paul Krugman's *The Age of Diminished Expectations* (Cambridge, Mass.: MIT Press, 1990), pp. 153–68.

WE HAVE A RIGHT TO A CLEAN ENVIRONMENT REGARDLESS OF COST

Everyone is talking about cleaning up the environment. Not only are they talking about it, they all want action. This is a far cry from a decade ago when environmental issues took a back seat to other social and economic priorities. Even corporations are jumping on the "green" bandwagon to help sell their products. There's almost unanimous agreement about the need to reduce waste, cut back noxious gas and chemical emissions, prevent the further erosion of the ozone layer, and clean up lakes and rivers. But are more regulations and tougher laws the answer? Are there other ways to protect the environment at a lower cost to society?

WHY POLLUTION EXISTS

Before answering that question, it is important to examine why there is a problem in the first place. Conventional thought is that unregulated markets cannot protect the environment. The theory goes something like this: air and water are "public" or "free" goods — that is, industries and individuals can use up as much as they want if they don't have to pay for them. Polluters don't consider the costs to society (known as externalities) of cleaning up the environment, just the direct costs of inputs in their production process.[1] An electricity-producing company worries only about how much it pays in wages, rent, interest and taxes, not how much it costs to clean up sulphur dioxide from burning coal. Why should they? As far as many of them are concerned, there's no incentive to do so. The atmosphere isn't like other factors of production. If the price of labour increases, there's a clear incentive to economize by hiring fewer workers and buying more machines. Because the atmosphere is in a sense a free good, the total price of producing energy in this case doesn't reflect the cost of a damaged environment. In the end society ends up paying the full cost with polluted air and water, greater health problems and a depletion of wildlife and vegetation. Without government intervention, the argument goes, unregulated free markets are incapable of protecting the environment.

There are a number of possible solutions. One is to pass laws that restrict certain pollutants, possibly by setting a minimum level of allowable pollution and leaving it up to individual companies to develop and pay for the necessary technology to meet these standards. We'll call this approach command and control. Industries are commanded by laws and controlled through careful monitoring. Most environmentalists approve of more regulations, along with stringent laws and stiffer penalties to force industries to cut back on pollution.

Another method, favoured by most economists, is to use market forces to encourage less pollution by putting a price on polluting the environment.[2] The idea, in other words, is to sell industry the right to pollute. This is where environmentalists and economists part ways. Environmentalists hold that the market can't be trusted to do the job; economists see the problem as a flaw in the market that can be corrected.

Regardless of which method is used to reduce pollution, we can't get rid of *all* pollution. A pollution-free society is impossible to achieve as long as industrial processes involve the use of raw materials. Legislation and government programs can't change the laws of physics. Economic theory proves that the more the amount of pollution is reduced, the more expensive it is to eliminate. In other words, the *marginal cost* goes up the more pollution we eliminate.[3]

Some argue that we should pay any price to get rid of all pollution and to move as close to point 0 in Figure 17.1 as possible. What if it cost 50 percent of the GNP to eliminate 90 percent of all air pollution? Is it worth the price? We might have cleaner air, but a lot less health care, education, and housing for the poor. Even if pollution threatens our health, it may make little sense to get rid of it all "at any cost". One Harvard physicist found that if a benzene standard proposed by the Occupational Safety and Health Adminstration (OSHA) was implemented, it might save one life at the cost of $300 million.[4] OSHA standards might make for a cleaner environment, but only at an extreme cost to society. If we want to save lives, there are cheaper and more efficient ways of doing it. A million dollars spent on smoke detectors saves almost 17 lives, better roads and guard rails save 50 lives, and screening for colon can-

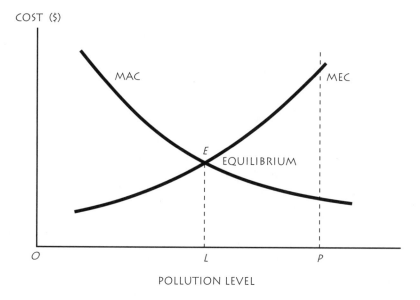

COST ($)

MAC

MEC

E
EQUILIBRIUM

O   L   P

POLLUTION LEVEL

NOTE: The graph above shows the cost of fighting pollution with abatement equipment and the external cost of pollution to our health and environment. The *Marginal Abatement Cost* (MAC) rises the closer we get to a zero level of pollution (right to left). The more pollution society produces, the higher the *Marginal External Cost* (MEC) — left to right. At a level of pollution *OP*, pollution is worth fighting because the benefits outweigh the costs. But not for pollution levels less than *OL* where costs are greater than the benefits to society. Where MAC and MEC cross at (*E*) is known as the *Efficient Level of Pollution.*

FIGURE 17.1   THE COSTS AND BENEFITS OF FIGHTING POLLUTION

cer 100 lives. Spending a million dollars on immunization in Indonesia saves around 10,000 lives.[5]

All of a sudden cleaning up the environment at "any price" seems less appealing. The question now becomes, how much pollution are we willing to tolerate and at what price?

WHY ENACTING MORE REGULATIONS DOES NOT ALWAYS WORK

Environmental activists argue that people have a right to clean air and water regardless of cost. Suppose we take the environmentalist's approach and impose the highest standards regarding water pollution and enforce these standards with tough fines and penalties.

Suppose one follows the line of action that threatens executives with jail if their company pollutes. It's not that this has not been done. But the existence of law is one thing, getting compliance to it is quite another. For example, almost twenty years after amendments to the Fisheries Act in 1971, only a few pulp and paper mills discharge effluents that are *not* lethal to fish — a direct violation of the intent of the act. Experience shows that if industry believes laws are unfair or too costly, they will fight them in court — and their chances of winning are pretty good. Under the Canadian Environment Protection Act, the federal government inspected 5,821 pollution violations from June 1988 to March 1990.[6] Yet, only two convictions resulted. It's hard to believe our environment was that clean.

There are many reasons why the command and control approach is ineffective. Complicated statutes have to be set in place. These could take years to implement. Regulatory agencies have to define precise standards and the best available technology to be used. Governments then have to hire an army of scientists to monitor the regulations and officials to enforce the laws. When cases eventually go to court, government regulators find themselves understaffed and overworked, going up against highly paid lawyers representing wealthy corporations. Even when violators are proven guilty, the fines are usually small compared with the damage done to the environment.[7] In short, the process of command and control is unnecessarily adversarial, costly to the taxpayer and inefficient.[8]

SELLING THE RIGHT TO POLLUTE

From an economic viewpoint, the problem can be treated completely differently. Instead of threatening the polluter with punitive penalties, the market is now used to reduce the level of pollution. The market system works in such a way that the government could sell a fixed number of permits to companies that would allow them to discharge a given level of pollutants. A company could pollute up to but not exceeding limits specified by the number of permits it is allowed to or is financially able to buy. Unused permits could then be sold on the secondary market. For example, if the marginal cost (the cost of eliminating an extra unit of pollution) for company A is $500 because it has the latest abatement equipment and $3,000 for company B which doesn't, the first company can make or save money by selling its pollution rights to company B. If the price of the permit is $2,000, company A gains $1500 ($2,000 – $500) while company B saves $1,000. Total savings to the economy is $2,500 ($1500 + $1,000). However if the price is above $3,000, it's less expensive for company B to invest in pollution abatement equipment, rather than buy a permit on the open market.

This system has three basic virtues. First, selling permits encourages firms to save money by reducing their emissions. If a company holds ten permits but needs only eight, it can sell its remaining permits to a less-efficient firm. Second, it rewards those firms using the best pollution technology and penalizes those that don't, saving society's resources. Third, if society wants to curtail pollution by 50 percent, it simply issues half the number of permits the next year.[7] By doing so it makes unused permits even more valuable thereby encouraging more companies to install better pollution equipment.[8] Under the existing process of strict government regulation, there's no incentive to clean up more than the law requires. If the law states that a firm can emit ten tonnes of goo into the river each year, there's no reason for that company spend a dime to decrease the amount of emissions. This is not so with market incentives.

What happens to less-efficient firms with outdated pollution controls? If they're allowed only ten permits but need eleven, for example, they'll have to buy the extra one from a firm that doesn't need it. The price for that extra permit will be determined by the market and the value of the permit will depend on how many were issued. The less-efficient polluter will keep buying permits as long as it's less expensive to do that than to acquire new equipment. Pollution permits reward firms that have modern pollution equipment and penalize those that use old technology.

In both the command and control approach and the market approach, the objectives are the same: to reduce overall pollution emissions. Under the command and control approach if everyone is required to reduce emissions by 50 percent, it's harder for a firm using the most modern technology than one with outdated methods because its marginal costs are higher than those of a less-efficient firm. Regulations tend to reward inefficiency while penalizing pollution-conscious companies. In other words, it provides the wrong incentives. With government controls there are no incentives to clean up more, whereas with permits freely traded on the market, it's in the interest of polluters to become more efficient. The chances of success are greater. Society wins two ways: less pollution and added tax revenues from the sale of the permits.[9]

Some environmentalists don't like the economist's solution because it smacks of a right to pollute. They argue that a rich company would simply buy permits to pollute. It could do this if its marginal cost of pollution abatement exceeded the price of the permit. Otherwise, the firm would be acting irrationally. Others believe that free markets don't work, or that firms aren't interested in saving money. There are centuries of experience and evidence to disprove the first criticism, and simple logic to counter the second.

Objections to the market approach don't die easily. Some argue that a price tag on air and water cheapens these things in the eyes of society or that a clean environment should be considered a right and not simply a way of saving money. To an economist, these lines of reasoning makes little sense. What's important are the results. Should society care how the environment is protected as long as we have cleaner air and water?[10]

USING TAXES TO DECREASE POLLUTION

Taxes can have the same results as permits. Some economists make the case that if taxes for each product are set at a level that just covers the social and private costs of production, then you have what is called allocative efficiency. In other words, the taxes raised would be spent to clean up the damage done to the environment. With permits, you know exactly how much pollution will result because governments control how many are issued. Taxes are a hit-and-miss proposition. If the objective is to reduce chemical emissions by three-and-a-half tonnes, taxes have to be estimated and firms monitored to gauge how they react to the tax. Taxes are then adjusted accordingly. In theory, the results are similar to permits but the process is costly and time consuming.

If issuing permits is such a great idea, why aren't governments moving in that direction? In fact they are. Years of regulatory failure have prompted some governments to change their ways. The U.S. government is using the free market approach by issuing permits to reduce air pollution in their new Clean Air Act. The program has been endorsed not only by economists, but by a number of environmental groups as well. The U.S. experience teaches that tradable permits work. A company that closes down or installs improved pollution-abatement equipment receives emission credits that it can sell. Illinois, California and Wisconsin have set up computer systems to keep track of credits nationwide. More of these central marketplaces will spring up as more states allow companies to pollute only if they have permits. Companies are being allowed to bank these emission permits for sale or use in the future. This gives them even more economic incentives to reduce pollution levels below what the law requires. Even in the fight to protect the ozone layer under an international agreement called the Montreal Protocol, transferring rights to producers and users of chlorofluoro-carbons (CFCs) and halons was the least expensive and most effective way to reduce these emissions. Both Environment Canada and the U.S. Environment Protection Agency support this approach.[11]

The Canadian government unfortunately decided to take a different tack with its 1990 Green Plan. Here it will spend $3 billion over five years to eliminate forty-four toxins and reduce waste by 50 percent by the year 2000 using more regulation and no market incentives. Ontario passed a new Environmental Protection Act in 1987 that raised the maximum fine on a company for polluting up to $50,000 a day and up to $250,000 a day for hazardous waste. The new act also calls for sending officials to jail if found guilty of willful pollution.[12] Will the plan work? One can only hope so, for the sake of the environment and the taxpayer. If past experience is any indicator, we'll end up with a dirtier environment and a less efficient economy.

NOTES

[1] Economists refer to damage to the environment as *externalities*, or an added cost to a third party or society. These costs usually arise when there's no private ownership of property; in this case air and water. If there was clear title, the owner could sue for damages. When there's no clear ownership, as with the environment, governments use other means to cope with externalities.

[2] Professor Alan S. Blinder in his book, *Hard Heads, Soft Hearts* (Reading, Mass.: Addison-Wesley, 1987), gives a lucid account of the economist's approach to the environment.

[3] A U.S. study by the Environmental Protection Agency (EPA) found that it would cost $60 billion U.S. to reduce effluent emissions by 85 to 90 percent, and an additional $200 billion U.S. to eliminate the remaining 10 to 15 percent. In other

words, the "marginal cost" of fighting pollution keeps rising. That's why "zero-tolerance," or getting rid of that "last ounce" of pollution is neither feasible nor economical.

4   Hard Heads Soft Hearts, pg 139.

5   Jane M. Orient, M.D., "Worried About TCE? Have Another Cup of Coffee" in Rational Reading On Environmental Concerns, Pg 188 edited by Jay H. Lehr, Van Nostrand Reinhold, New York, 1992. It's estimated that spending $1 million on sulphur scrubbers in power plants saves approximately two lives.

6   Since the mid 1970s, The Department of the Environment has been responsible for twenty-six environmental acts. By 1988 only ten cases were prosecuted under the Canada Water Act, the Environmental Contamination Act, the Clean Air Act, and the Ocean Dumping Control Act. In many cases it wasn't even clear which level of government had jurisdiction.

7   In 1985 Dow Chemical Company of Sarnia was fined a total of $16,000 for four violations, after months of investigations, for dumping tar into the St. Clair River. This was hardly a burden to Dow. Ford Canada was fined $5,000 on three counts of spilling oil into the Detroit River under the Ontario Water Resources Act in 1988.

8   In all fairness, there have been some successes using this approach in Canada. Sulphur dioxide emissions are down 60 percent over the past fifteen years but at a cost of $1.5 billion to the taxpayer and industry. Ontario Hydro estimates it can comply with rigid provincial abatement measures by the turn of the century at a cost of $2.5 billion. The question now arises, can society achieve similar or better results at a lower cost?

9   Who gets to buy the permits can be determined by a number of criteria including share of output in an industry. The permit system will also be policed, but when a firm is found polluting beyond its limit, it will be fined according to set penalties with no court action.

10   The market system would not work with highly dangerous toxins. In such cases the only acceptable means of control is a complete ban.

11   It is estimated by the EPA that the United States spends over $70 billion a year on reducing pollution. Studies show that using the market approach could save up to $50 billion without increasing the level of pollution.

12   Odd as it may seem, some industries prefer regulations to free markets when it comes to pollution control. They know their costs under regulations, but not under the pollution permit system. One argument is that they cannot know the value of their permits when it comes time to sell.

13   Douglas A. Smith, "The Implementation of Canadian Policies to Protect the Ozone Layer," in G. Bruce Doern (ed.), *Getting It Green* (Toronto: C.D. Howe Institute, 1990), p. 111.

14   The C. D. Howe Institute has given the Green Plan high marks on intent, but low marks on process because it fails to use "market approaches as a complement to traditional regulation"—see G. Bruce Doern, *Shade of Green: Gauging Canada's Green Plan* (Toronto: C.D. Howe Institute, 1990), p. 10.

WE ARE RUNNING OUT OF NONRENEWABLE RESOURCES

N o one can argue with the fact that the world has limited resources. The earth's resources are fixed by nature. We therefore live in a finite world. On this point there is no dispute. But many people make the false assumption that because we have only so much oil, minerals and agricultural growing capacity that some day, if we keep consuming as we are today, we'll wake up and find we have run out of some vital resource. After all, it only stands to reason that with the world's per capita consumption continuing to go up, especially in the West, and with a growing global population, the well will eventually run dry. Although the first premise of finite resources is true, it is a myth to conclude that the world will run out of any resources whether they are renewable resources, such as agriculture or nonrenewable resources, such as minerals. What will save the earth's resources from being exhausted? The answer lies partly in the working of the price system. Let's take a look at why this myth is so predominant in our thinking about resources, and then we'll examine how a free market system works to ensure that the earth's resources won't disappear.

IT ALL BEGAN WITH REVEREND MALTHUS

The belief that the world was on a collision course with nature began in the late eighteenth century when Reverend Thomas Robert Malthus predicted that population growth would grow beyond the capabilities of agriculture to feed it, resulting in widespread famine and death. Although his dreaded forecasts never materialized, that did not stop modern day Cassandras from following in his footsteps, not the least of which were those who forecast the dire projections of the Club of Rome report in 1972. This neo-Malthusian group made up of European and American academics used computer models to forecast how exponential economic growth would exhaust the world's resources in the next couple of decades if we kept consuming at the rate that we were when their report, *The Limits of Growth*, was published. The Club of Rome's report got a lot of publicity and created substantial controversy. The fact that the forecasts were discredited did not make much difference. Ironically, the study made the same errors Malthus made. First, it ignored the advance of technology; once this crucial oversight is taken into account, the dire predictions disappear. Second, it failed to take into account the fact that people, industry and governments change their behaviour when prices rise.

Just earlier than this other pessimists were also issuing dire warnings. In 1968 Paul Ehrlich, a famous ecologist and professor at Stanford University wrote in his book, *The Population Boom*, that the population growth in the world was outstripping the world's supply of food, fresh water and minerals. He used the ecological concept of carrying capacity to argue that the earth could support only so much population growth. Again the idea is the same one advocated by the Malthusians. Ehrlich painted a bleak future for the human race if it did not change its ways. He went on to say in his later book, *The End of Affluence*, that due to a combination of ignorance, greed and callousness, a situation has been created that could lead a billion or more people to starve. He predicted that before 1985 mankind will enter a genuine age of scarcity in which "the accessible supply of many key resources will be nearing depletion."[1] He predicted rising food prices as food production bumped up against the limits of a world with diminishing capacity for more agricultural output.

Ehrlich remained so sure that the world was using up all its resources that in 1980 he predicted that by 1990 the price of most minerals would go up. In a well-publicized bet with the economist Julian Simon, who predicted the opposite would happen, Ehrlich chose five minerals: nickel, copper, tin, chrome, and tungsten. By the end of 1990, the price of each mineral had fallen in real dollar terms. Simon won the bet.[2]

THE PRICE SYSTEM TO THE RESCUE

Why is it that a growing population, an increase in incomes and GDP, and the highest level of consumption ever experienced in history do not come even near to depleting the world's resources? Some argue, as Ehrlich does, that we just don't know how much oil, copper, and other minerals are in the ground but that in time, prices will rise as we get closer to the limit. A more fundamental explanation, however, resides in the working of free markets and the price system. Here is how it works: whenever a shortage of a resource is created by an increase in demand, or a decrease in supply, the price of that product goes up. It's a simple matter of supply and demand. That part is straightforward. The interesting thing is how markets react to rising prices. Forecasters who project dire consequences assume we go on consuming regardless of the cost until the resources disappear. But when prices rise, three things tend to happen in varying degrees: we consume less, look for less-expensive alternatives, and search for more. The prediction of the Club of Rome's report wasn't lost on the OPEC cartel when they quadrupled the price of oil in the early 1970s. In 1979 the price of oil was six times its level in 1973, as energy analysts saw prices of over $100 U.S. a barrel by the end of the decade. What followed should be a lesson to anyone who doubts the working of the price system.[3]

In the short term little could be done about rising oil prices except to pay the higher bill. In time, oil-dependent nations in the West responded as any rational consumer would by using relatively less-expensive, alternative energy forms, such as hydro, natural gas and nuclear power. The more marginal energy sources (e.g., solar, wind and methane gas) also came into their own as their relative costs compared to petroleum began to drop. Consumers began demanding smaller, more fuel-efficient cars, became involved in energy conservation, and generally weaned themselves away from expensive Middle East petroleum. Industry began adopting more energy-efficient technologies and shutting down wasteful energy manufacturing.[4] Even though GDP per capita rose 21 percent from 1973 to 1986 in OECD countries, energy per capita dropped by 6 percent over the same period. The developed countries were adjusting to higher oil prices. All these actions had the desired effect. By 1986 the real price of oil (after inflation) was at the pre-1973 oil shock level.[5] This stunning turn of events sent OPEC reeling as the cartel members broke rank and began undercutting each other hoping to hold on to diminishing markets.

As prices rose during the 1970s, the profit motive kicked in as billions of dollars were invested in searching for new oil. In 1970 the known reserves of oil stood at 34.8 years (see Table 18.1); by 1990 that had increased to 43.4 years. Natural gas reserves, which

Fuel	1970	1990
Oil	34.8	43.4
Natural Gas	44.6	58.2
Coal	N/A	238.0

Source: "Energy and the Environment," The Economist (31 August 1991), p. 4.

TABLE 18.1 NUMBER OF PROVEN YEARS OF SELECTED FUEL RESERVES REMAINING

are a by-product of oil exploration, also increased from 44.6 years to 58.2 over the same twenty years.[6] It is estimated that recoverable reserves of all forms of fossil fuels may be 650 times current annual consumption worldwide. Because of these massive reserves, new energy forms, and conservation, the International Energy Agency does not expect the price of oil to go beyond $40 U.S. during the first quarter of the next century. The supply of energy has proven to be much more responsive to price changes than many believed. In the language of economics the elasticity of supply for oil is higher in the long run. The higher the price, the more oil comes on stream, and that means prices cannot stay high for long.

If the price should rise higher, there is still plenty of scope for conservation that will keep the price of energy in check. This is one area where there are substantial gains to be made. One Canadian study found that conservation had big payback for businesses. Companies could save the equivalent of $22 U.S. a barrel by investing $13 in energy conservation. Dow Chemical, for example, found that it pays to conserve. In 1988 the company invested around $22 million in over ninety-five energy saving projects. That investment earned them a return of 190 percent.

One can also make the argument that the billions of dollars invested over the years in alternative energy form, such as nuclear fusion, led to the scientific breakthrough that could one day see a new kind of energy that is inexpensive, clean and virtually inexhaustible.[7] Because the major fusion fuel, deuterium (an isotope of hydrogen) can be easily extracted from water in endless quantities, fusion could produce far more energy from the "top two inches of Lake Erie than exists in all the earth's known oil reserves."[8] With that promise, we may see the end of the world energy problem within a hundred years.[9] Technological advances are also preserving other nonrenewable resources. Where copper once was used to transmit digital information over great distances, fibre optics have greater capacity to carry voice and digital information at lower cost. The raw material for fibre optics and semiconductors is common sand; a resource in endless supply. In this sense there are no finite natural resources.

The main lesson for governments in preserving resources, or encouraging their development, is that prices should be allowed to move freely so that the balance between supply and demand can be maintained. Governments should not intervene in markets under the misguided impression that by keeping the price of a resource below market price it is increasing the welfare of its citizens. Consider the cases of Eastern Europe and the former Soviet Union. In their effort to catch up to the West, they kept the price of fossil fuels below the cost of exploration, refining, and distribution. This led to a monumental waste of oil and coal because there was no incentive to economize. In China the situation is even worse. China uses twice as much energy to produce one unit of GDP as Russia and four times as much as Japan.[10] Russia is now undergoing a painful economic transition by increasing its price of oil to world levels after years of subsidizing the consumption of fossil fuels. When nonrenewable resources are kept below world prices through government policy, it leads to waste and inefficiency. As long as the price system is allowed to work unimpeded, there should be little worry that the world's resources will soon run out.

NOTES

[1]   As quoted by John Tierney in "Betting the Planet," *New York Times Magazine* (2 December 1990), p. 76.

[2]   Ehrlich still thinks that the price of these minerals will increase but ten years was not enough time for shortages to make themselves apparent. Simon was still willing to take Ehrlich's bet See John Tierney, "Betting the Planet," *The New York Times Magazine* (2 December 1990), p. 52.

[3]   It would be naive to assume that all of the earth's resources can be preserved as long as the price system operates freely in an open market. Exceptions are the wholesale destruction of the Brazilian rain forest and wildlife. In such cases waiting for price adjustments in order to change human behaviour may be too slow and inefficient to save precious species. In such cases nothing short of a worldwide ban and strict enforcement will do.

⁴ Countries that have a higher standard of living tend to encourage those industries that are more energy efficient. For example, an aluminum smelter spends $1.20 on energy for every dollar allocated to wages and capital, while a producer of inorganic chemicals (oxygen or chlorine) spends $0.25 on energy. A computer manufacturer spends only 1.5 cents. OECD countries moved away from energy-intensive industries to more energy-efficient ones. See "Energy and the Environment," *The Economist* (31 August 1991), p. 130.

⁵ As the current price of oil is around $20 U.S. it looks as if the oil in the Alberta tar sands will remain there for a long time. It is feasible to recover only if the price hits $60 a barrel.

⁶ To put these figures in more historical perspective, the world's known oil reserves stood at 100 billion barrels in 1950; by 1970 they had risen to 550 billion barrels, and by 1990, to over 1 trillion barrels. See "Energy and the Environment," *The Economist*.

⁷ "Breakthrough in Nuclear Fusion Offers Hope for Power of Future," *The New York Times* (11 November 1991), section 1, p. 1. The article goes on to say that nuclear fusion could be commercially feasible within fifty years.

⁸ "Breakthrough in Nuclear Fusion."

⁹ Another promising area of a limitless energy source is the sun. It's estimated that the production of chemical fuels generated from the sun can easily deliver upward of 450 exajoules a year (one exajoule being equivalent to the energy released by 22 million tons of oil). The process requires converting sunlight to a chemical that can be stored and shipped. The problem is that this promising solar technology is underfunded. In IEA countries 60 percent of R&D for energy goes to nuclear power, and only 4 percent to solar and biomass. See Israel Dostrovsky, "Chemical Fuels from the Sun," *Scientific American*, December 1991. See also "Energy and the Environment," *The Economist*.

¹⁰ "Energy and the Environment," *The Economist*.

RECYCLING ALWAYS MAKES
GOOD BUSINESS SENSE

here are few programs that have caught the public's willing-
ness to preserve the environment as much as the waste recycling program. The process seems so logical: if we could
recover, sort and recycle the millions of tonnes of material we now
put into landfill, we would put less pressure on the environment.
The whole system would eventually be self-financing because the
waste would be sold as inputs into the production of goods we now
buy. It is such an appealing idea that thousands of communities
have started curb-side collection programs of bottles, cans, plastics
and old newspapers. The idea seemed too good to be true.

Unfortunately, as with most good intentions, recycling had
two major shortcomings: first, the costs of collecting, sorting and
shipping recycled waste was greater than what business was willing
to pay for the waste, which made it a bad business proposition; and
second, the environmental benefits did not turn out to be what had
been anticipated. What was supposed to be a win-win proposition,
ended up as a lose-lose situation instead. What went wrong? Critics
of Blue Box programs claimed that the participants were on a collision course with the economics of the situation from the start, and
that it was never realistic to assume that recycling would pay for
itself.

However, it wasn't economics that was the impediment, but
rather ill-thought-out programs that misused economic principles.
Before getting into the details of what went wrong and what to do
about it, it is important to examine insights that economics may
provide about the recycling process.

GOOD INTENTIONS: BAD ECONOMICS

The economic system produces waste at each stage of the production process: when resources are extracted from the earth; at the production stage; and finally when products are used up and eventually discarded as litter, sewage or garbage. In nature, on the other hand, since everything is eventually recycled there is no such built-in tendency to waste in the production process. Traditionally the science of economics has said nothing about waste because it carried a zero price. In other words, the effective cost of polluting the environment was too low to bother about. But as the damage to the environment became more obvious, we began attaching real value to the environment, not only aesthetically, but also as an assimilator or repository for waste. What happens when we start to run out of landfills, or discarded rubbish washes back to shore, or toxic waste leaches through the ground is that real harm is being done to the earth, and its capacity to absorb the waste is shrinking. This is not the fault of economics or economists, as some environmental critics claim, but ignorance of the true cost of production.

Recycling was seen as a panacea to the problems of waste in modern society — if we could only recover everything we throw out, we could save the environment and keep the world's resources intact. However, there are two fundamental reasons why this line of reasoning won't work. The first reason has to do with something called entropy.[1] This means that not everything can be recycled or reused. Of the millions of commodities and products used in the economy, the majority dissipate throughout the economic system. For example, think of the impossibility of recapturing lead in leaded gasoline after it has been used. Even if we recapture the carbon dioxide from burning fossil fuel, we cannot make another energy form out of it. Junked cars have little to give up in terms of recyclable materials: the lead in car batteries is generally recycled, but the wood and plastics are almost impossible to extract without spending large and unfeasible amounts of money. Entropy puts a physical limit on creating a closed economic system. We have to live with the reality that not all the waste at each stage of production can be reused or recycled.

The second reason has to do with cost. Untold millions of tonnes of materials are thrown out because it's just too expensive to recover them given the current market conditions and demands. In economic terms, the marginal costs surpass the marginal revenue of recycled material recovery. This second factor goes to the heart of the recycling crisis: it is simply not worth the price unless policies are in place to encourage the purchase and use of recycled material in the production process. Furthermore, it makes no sense to collect, sort and sell recycled material at less than the cost of collecting it. In Toronto it costs between $200 to $300 per tonne to collect recycled materials compared to $50 for regular garbage. The net cost to Toronto taxpayers is $193 per tonne (cost of collection minus the value of the materials collected).[2] Some claim that these costs are worth paying to protect the environment but others are willing to pay only for programs that work and are effective. The way it stands now, municipalities find themselves warehousing mountains of newsprint, cans, bottles and plastics with no markets in which to sell them. Municipalities cannot go on subsidizing curb-side collection indefinitely. It is not only the public sector that is losing money. Private companies that went into the recycling business hoping to profit from the need and public demand to recycle are also losing.

One problem is that the price of recycled materials has been falling, making the whole process more expensive to the taxpayer. In 1991 glass brought $60 a tonne; today it yields about $40. Metro Toronto gets about $16 a tonne for newsprint, down from $30. Recycled steel brings in only $77 a tonne, $115 less than the cost of collecting it from households. The lower the price that governments get for recycled material, the higher the cost to the tax payer.[3]

The absurdity is that much of this material for one reason or another ends up in landfill anyway. Glass companies are very picky about the colour of glass they want; the rest is dumped. Toronto has already cut back its Blue Box program because of cost problems, so again, much of the material is dumped. Given our limited resources, there have to be less-expensive and more-effective ways to cut down on waste to the benefit of taxpayers *and* nature.[4]

Banning products outright is not always the solution either. In the case of plastics, it may end up doing more harm than good. For example, McDonald's bowed to public pressure to eliminate its polystyrene containers but the paper wrappings they are now using may end up doing the environment even more harm.[5] The same anomaly arose with diapers. It's assumed by some that cloth diapers are better than disposables because they can be used over and over. But in a study done by Arthur D. Little, a Boston consulting firm, it was found that cloth diapers actually end up costing the environment more in water and energy consumption, and in air pollution than the disposables do.[6]

THE LIMITS OF RECYCLING

If we all agree that because of the laws of physics not everything can be recycled, and the laws of economics dictate that not everything should be recycled if cheaper ways can be found to solve the waste problem, can we still save the environment? The answer is yes, and following are some of the solutions.

User Pay Programs

The first goal of any policy to cut down on the amount of waste produced by society is to get at the root causes of the problem, and that means making polluters (businesses as well as households) pay the true costs of waste disposal. Programs that simply collect bottles and cans regardless of how much is tossed out have no incentive to cut down on waste disposal. If taxes are fixed, households assume that garbage collection is free and act accordingly. They may feel better about recycling, but the real costs are just passed along elsewhere. On the other hand, if consumers are forced to pay for the paper or materials they now throw out, they will demand less of it from manufacturers.

Some American cities are experimenting with charging people according to how much they throw out. Although there are some problems with this approach (such as tossing garbage over the neighbour's fence or along a roadside at night), the results in places like Tocoma and Seattle, Washington, look promising. People are throwing out less garbage. If consumers are not held to account, they have no reason to demand less packaging or returnable containers from businesses. The way we now pursue waste reduction and recycling, everyone loses — governments, consumers, corporations, communities and the environment — and the problem is getting worse.

The question of who owns the waste goes to the heart of the matter. Some environmentalists make the claim that corporations should be responsible for disposing of the products they sell after they have been used. This is actually the premise for a law in Germany, for example, that compels retailers to take back packaging from consumers, and manufacturers to then retrieve it from retailers, and so on down the line until 80 percent of it is recycled. The problem is that the program is horrendously expensive and the only one that will end up paying is the consumer as companies pass along the costs.

Market Forces and Waste Reduction

As environmentalists have often stressed, recycling is just one way to cut down on waste disposal. A far more effective means is to discourage waste in the first place. The free market already has built-in incentives to cut down on waste by producing lighter packages that reduce material and shipping costs. The U.S. National Center for Policy Analysis found that plastic milk jugs weighing ninety-five grams in the early 1970s, today weigh only sixty grams. Competitive markets have also cut back the weight of twelve-ounce steel cans by 65 percent, and aluminum cans by 35 percent over the past three decades (see Figure 19.1). In order to encourage more reduction and less waste, it's important that corporations are not subsidized in the use of virgin raw materials. Recycling cannot hope to compete in these cases. Policies that make virgin materials less expensive to use range from provisions for writing off the costs of finding minerals and fuels to favourable capital gains treatment for an industry such as logging. One industry in which recycling has actually made a business more competitive is cardboard box manu-

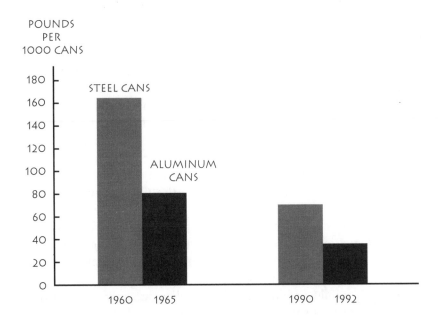

Source: U.S. National Center for Policy Analysis, Investors Business Daily (29 November 1991).

FIGURE 19.1   MARKETS DO NOT WAIT TO USE RESOURCES EFFICIENTLY

facturing. By using recycled content, it has helped Canada's producers save on virgin wood fibre and chemicals, and allowed it to lower costs and compete against low-cost U.S. producers.[7]

One way governments can encourage the market to produce less waste is to use their procurement programs to buy only from firms that achieved certain waste reduction standards or purchased products with a set amount of recycled material. Another way would be to create a program that would encourage newspapers to use more recycled fibre by setting a national target, and then allowing papers that beat it to sell their spare share to others that failed to meet it. In the final analysis, the most effective policy is for governments to set goals and limits for waste reduction and let the market determine the most efficient means of reaching those goals. This is one area where the judicious use of government regulation may do more good than harm.

Landfills and Incinerators

One of the least-appreciated solutions to the waste problem is the use of landfills. The perception is that garbage dumps are stinking heaps of toxic waste. Actually, they are generally benign.[8] Filling them with glass and other non-biodegradable material is not a threat to the environment. Philosophically it would be hard to differentiate between putting a bottle or a rock into the ground. Any real distinction would be based on nothing other than sentimentality.

Regardless of how much we recycle and reuse, there will always be a growing need for landfills that have to be relatively close to population centres. One way to get over the fear of them is to have municipalities see them (and promote them to their citizens) as a source of income. This is an effective way to get over the not-in-my-back-yard syndrome. In 1991, the Ontario government refused to allow the city of Toronto to sell its garbage to Kirkland Lake where it would be dumped in a safe, open-pit mine on the dubious logic that waste should stay where it's made as a matter of principle.[9] However, we are not running out of safe places to put landfills. It is estimated that all of America's garbage for the next 1,000 years would fit into a single landfill space only 120 feet deep and 44 miles square.[10]

Incinerating our waste has long been opposed by environmentalists for the valid reason that toxic pollutants are no better for humans than they are for the environment. But incineration technology that turns waste into energy has improved making it environmentally safer when materials are burned at extremely high temperatures. In Sweden, where this is done, plastics are know as "white coal." Although some experts do not like burning plastics (or other waste) for energy on the grounds that it does not produce as much energy as it takes to make the plastic product in the first place, it should not be overlooked as a promising form of waste control.

In the final analysis, recycling is only one method that can be used to cut down on waste, and often it is not the most cost-effective. Policies that assume everything can be recycled, regardless of the cost and without incentive programs to encourage guaranteed supply of recycled material and its use, are doomed to fail. Today everyone recognizes the value of cutting back on waste for the benefit of the environment. It would be a shame to dissipate that cooperative spirit with misguided government programs.

Finally, who should pay for it? The consumer who initially buys the goods or the producer who makes them in the first place? The answer is, both. For recycling to work, incentives have to be used to encourage consumers to cut consumption of recyclable material; and programs have to be set up to make it economically viable for corporations to use more recycled material. Simply collecting cans, bottles and newspapers without a well-thought-out scheme of what to do with them and how to do it only leads to waste and higher municipal taxes.

NOTES

[1] Entropy is often known as the Second Law of Thermodynamics. See David W. Pearce and R. Kerry Turner, *Economics of Natural Resources and the Environment* (Baltimore: Johns Hopkins University Press, 1990), p. 38.

[2] These numbers are according to the Metropolitan Toronto Department of Works. See *The Globe and Mail* (5 March 1992), p. A15.

[3] Kruger Inc. of Montreal, which actually gets its old newspapers for free from the city of Albany N.Y., gets only $7 a tonne for it on the market which doesn't even cover the cost of bailing. See *The Globe and Mail* (23 December 1991), p. B3.

[4] In 1992, Metro Toronto will landfill about $1 million dollars worth of newspapers because of a paper strike at a paper plant in Southern Ontario. The Province of Ontario also subsidized the shipping of newsprint to South Korea and Nigeria, at considerable expense to the taxpayer, during the strike. See *The Financial Times of Canada* (3 February 1992), p. 4.

5   Perhaps the most celebrated incident of public pressure to recycle is the case of McDonald's restaurants. The company came under extreme pressure to ban its polystyrene hamburger clamshells even though it was planning to undergo a massive recycling program for the polystyrene. But the public would have none of it, and McDonald's finally relented and switched to paper wrappings. (The company could only take so many letters to "Ronald McToxic" from school children. The kids may have felt they were helping the environment, but that's not what happened.) It's true that McDonald's waste going to landfills dropped by 70 percent, but plastics make up only 16 percent of all landfill material and are relatively benign because they don't degrade or leach into the ground. McDonald's switch to paper killed an initiative to find ways to recycle the plastics from the thousands of restaurants throughout North America. Without a steady supply of plastics, companies are reluctant to invest in recycling programs. More important, paper wrappings are far less efficient as a thermal insulator which means greater food spoilage, and eventually more landfill needs. See George C. Lodge and Jeffrey F. Rayport, "Knee-Deep and Rising: America's Recycling Crisis," *Harvard Business Review*, September–October 1991.

6   Michael Fumento, "Recycling's Dubious Economics," *Investor's Business Daily* (29 November 1991), p. 2.

7   Kimberly Noble, "Box industry stands up to heavy odds," *The Globe and Mail* (7 September 1992), p. B1.

8   Landfills are composed mainly of paper (40 percent). Plastics only account for 16 percent and another 20 percent comes from building materials, which are almost impossible to recycle. See William Rathje and Cullen Murphy, "The Truth about Trash", *Smithsonian* (July 1992), p. 119

9   To help subsidize the expensive Blue Box program, landfill dumping fees were raised from $83.33 a tonne to $150 a tonne. The result was predictable. The volume of garbage dumped by private companies fell from 1.7 million tonnes in 1989, to less than one million tonnes by 1992. This will be a loss of $131 million in lost revenues. Ontario garbage is being taken to cheaper dump sites in the United States where our refuse is more welcome. The Minister of the Environment, Ruth Grier, is fighting to get our garbage back. See William Thorsell, "Solutions to the Waste Problem: A Question of Garbage In, Garbage Out," *The Globe and Mail* (7 March 1992).

'NO-GROWTH' WILL SAVE THE ENVIRONMENT

F ew would dispute the claim that modern life has had devastating effects on the environment. Without economic growth there would not be an ozone problem, toxic dumps like Love Canal, rain forests slowly burning away, lead poisoning in school yards, ever-expanding landfill sights, acid rain, dead lakes, the *Exxon Valdez* oil spill, and Chernobyl. None of these environmental tragedies would be possible without our craving for greater economic growth and higher standards of living. With ever-growing world population levels, the only solution seems to be stopping economic growth. It is easy to understand where the notion that slowing the population and economy's growth rate would save the planet. If growth is the problem, then no-growth is the answer. But is stopping *all* growth the best solution? Will the world be a cleaner, safer place if we put the brakes on economic development? The short answer is, probably not. The no-growth solution may actually make things worse.

WANTS VS. NEEDS

The basic premise of the no-growth school is that economic growth cannot be sustained indefinitely in view of the natural limits of the ecosystem. Economic growth, and an improvement in the standard of living, are incompatible with a healthy environment. Those who advocate that we turn off the lights, shut the taps and pull the plug on modern society argue that since growth is based on corporations selling us products we really do not need in order to maximize their own profits, then the destruction of the environment is unnecessary at best and unconscionable at worst. Besides, given that GDP increases cannot be sustained indefinitely because resources are limited, we should stop now because of the damage being done to the ecosystem. Environmentalists, such as Dr. David Suzuki, go as far as to blame economics itself for instilling the false values of profits, consumerism and greed. They argue that free markets are incapable of delivering products people demand, and that it is a myth to believe that consumers, through their spending power, get the products they need.[1]

The no-growth school also argues that even if we could produce all the goods we wanted, what could we possibly do with them all? Dr. Suzuki believes that "the human intellect cannot endlessly find new resources or create alternatives because the Earth is finite."[2] There's a notion that the world's resources are somehow limited (see Chapter 18). Even if resources are in short supply, the creativity and imagination to use them are not. Technology transforms our lives in ways no one can predict with certainty. Who could have imagined that today's humble and ubiquitous home computer that is used to store recipes and help children with their homework is faster than the largest computer used in the Pentagon after the Second World War? One day our great-grandchildren may look back in amazement that we used fossil fuels for energy, or that we did not have the knowledge to cure cancer, heart disease or AIDS.

Those who want to stop growth have a nostalgic view of the past as being a simpler, better time, without the stresses and strains of modern life, when people were more in harmony with their environment. Nothing is further from the truth. It was common for people to die of food poisoning before chemical additives brought safe food to the reach of millions. Only a century ago, the streets of major cities around the world were covered in disease-carrying manure. Those who justifiably want to cut down on needless packaging forget that it greatly reduces food spoilage and waste. In fact, the average Mexican household throws away three times more food than do North American households — they throw away more than half the amount of food required to provide an adult with a nutritionally balanced diet, all because of a lack of proper storage and packaging. It was the internal combustion engine that got rid of the manure pollution, which led to a quantum increase in the volume of traffic before new environmental problems arose. In time, new technologies will replace fossil fuels as a way to move traffic and people. Just as products and corporations have their life cycles, technologies also go through the stages of birth, growth and eventually death.[3]

The advocates of zero-growth have little or no faith in the economic concept of consumer sovereignty or, in other words, the ability of the consumer to dictate to the producer, through the market, what is produced. But corporations are joining the environmental thrust largely because consumers want environmentally safe products, less packaging, and more natural foods. Consumers, not corporations, are demanding these things; and corporations are listening, adapting and anticipating. Anyone who hasn't noticed this trend simply isn't paying attention. Environmental consciousness will only get stronger as the next generation demands even more changes to how we consume and dispose of our waste.

THE COST AND CONSEQUENCES OF NO-GROWTH

Even if growth could be stopped, there is no guarantee that people or the environment would be better off. If the Victorians had taken the same attitude and stopped growth, future generations would have been deprived of a ten-fold increase in the standard of living, and the advances in dentistry, open-heart surgery, antibiotics, birth control, central heating, personal computers, jet travel, and a thousand other things we take for granted in a modern world. Then there are all the social advances. It is hard to image women's liberation without the advances in technology that made many of the tasks associated with parenting and housekeeping so much faster and easier.[4] It's odd how we can marvel at the advances we have made over the last century but have little faith that we can continue to make advances in the future. Part of the problem is that we see future goods as being static, or more of the same, rather than as being new products satisfying new needs. Freezing growth impedes the creation of wealth on which research depends to advance science and technology. One cannot assume that without a growing economy technical progress will continue without interruption.

By slowing the economy we will be hampering the necessary scientific advances needed to solve the environmental problems. Despite all the bad news about the environment, there have been significant success stories, and most of them are due to scientific breakthroughs. In OECD countries over the past twenty years, urban levels of sulphur dioxide have fallen by 30 to 75 percent, airborne dust and grit by 40 to 50 percent, and lead concentrations by 85 percent in North American cities (see Figure 20.1). Twenty years ago Lake Erie was a horror story; now it has been brought back to

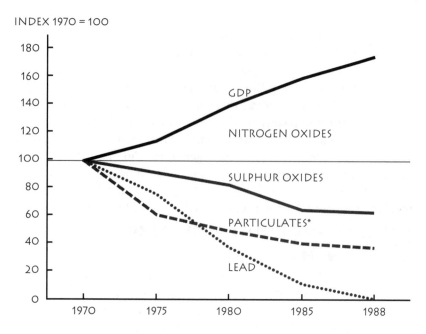

INDEX 1970 = 100

180
160
140 — GDP
120 — NITROGEN OXIDES
100
80 — SULPHUR OXIDES
60
40 — PARTICULATES*
20 — LEAD
0

1970   1975   1980   1985   1988

+ U.S. only
* Germany, Italy, Holland, U.K. & U.S.

Sources: World Development Report, adapted by The Economist (23 May 1992), p.79.

FIGURE 20.1   GROWTH DOES NOT ALWAYS MEAN MORE POLLUTION
(GDP AND EMISSIONS IN OECD COUNTRIES)

life and is the largest commercial fishery in the Great Lakes. Lakes once thought dead because of acid rain can be brought back to life. Sulphur dioxide emissions in Canada will drop from a high of almost 6 million tonnes in 1970 to under 2.5 tonnes by 1994.[5] Programs to clean up the environment cost industry and the tax payer billions of dollars that would not be available if the economy was not creating the necessary wealth. Much of the environmental damage, such as toxic dumps, the safe disposal of PCBs, and the removal of asbestos and lead contamination are mistakes of the past that will take billions of dollars to rectify. Where will the money for these clean-up jobs come from if not from a growing economy?[6] Also, there are years of research needed to switch from fossil fuels to solar power.

While billions will be needed to clean up the mistakes of the past, more will probably be needed for the world's biggest environmental problem: global warming or the greenhouse effect. The world now consumes the equivalent of 160 million barrels of oil each day. By 2010, two billion more people will be on the planet increasing energy consumption by another 50 to 60 percent. The pressures and damage to the environment will be enormous. But it is hard to see how slowing growth in the West could solve the global warming problem, given that the main growth in carbon-dioxide output will come from developing countries (where the additional two billion people will be). It will come as no surprise if these countries resist any international treaty that calls for a slowdown in their energy consumption while they are trying to catch up with the developed world.[7] Unfortunately two of world's most populated countries, China and India, will look to coal for their energy, since they have so much of it.

Coal still generates over half the world's electricity, more than any other fuel. Not only are developing countries more dependent on coal than the West, they use it less efficiently. Because the Third World and former socialist countries do not know how to properly price fuel, such as electricity, the World Bank estimates that they use 10 to 20 percent more than they need. State of the art technology exists to remove 95 percent of the sulphur dioxide from coal-fired stations, 99 percent of the ash and 90 percent of the nitrogen oxides. The main drawback is money. The question, then, is how to get the Third World to use less energy, save the environment, and still improve their standard of living. There are no easy answers, but two possible options are to transfer the latest Western technology, or literally to pay developing countries not to pollute. Asking them to adhere voluntarily to some international pollution quota is a nonstarter and sure to fail. In short, economic growth will be needed to: first, create the wealth to clean up past environmental and pollution hazards; second, encourage more R & D in alternative energy sources; and third, raise the standard of living in the Third World without destroying the world's environment.

OTHER REASONS GROWTH IS NEEDED

People's interest in protecting nature and the environment is also related to their standard of living. Those with higher incomes are more interested in environmental issues. The "slash and burn" practices currently destroying the rain forests of the Amazon jungle are the result of poverty and ignorance. That is why the UN-sponsored

Brundtland Report recommended the concept of sustainable development, the idea that growth and protecting the environment were not diametrically opposed, was the only viable option available. To meet the needs of the world's poor, a five to ten times increase in economic activity was necessary.[8] One cannot expect nations that can hardly feed themselves to be concerned with how they might mistreat the earth's ecosystem. The real threat to developing countries is not foreseeable environmental distress but poverty today, which according to the World Bank kills 34 million people a year, more than the population of Canada. Slowing economic growth will not improve their chances of living. By some estimates, once a country's per capita income rises above $4,000 U.S., it produces less pollutants per capita because it can afford technology such as catalytic converters and sewage treatment facilities. (Water pollution kills more people than global warming). Countries like Mexico and Russia are at that $4,000 threshold now. It is an odd morality that trades away helping the poor today so as to help unknown generations in the future by keeping resources in the ground and stopping economic growth. With a rising standard of living it becomes possible to increase the amount of education available to Third World countries. And there is a close relationship between more education and family size: women with a high school education in developing countries have an average of three children, while those without average seven.

Those who argue for growth for its own sake would be just as wrong as those who want no-growth. We are not talking about a mindless increase in GDP without regard for the kind of growth that is generated. That may have been the way of the 1960s, but not of the 1990s and beyond. The quality of production that is consistent with a healthy environment is better than simply increasing GDP, regardless of what comes at the other end. Growth is too often seen as a mindless increase in more shopping malls, more factories making products no one needs or wants ad infinitum. But there is no reason to fear growth that uses technology to produce products and services that improve the quality of life. What's needed are policies that promote full employment, and the kind of growth that minimizes the damage to the environment and also allows for a more equal distribution of income.

NOTES

1   This notion that there is a difference between *wants* and *needs* was popularized by the economist John Kenneth Galbraith in his book *The Affluent Society*. We need goods like food, shelter, clothing and education, but we want Big Macs, Giorgio Armani suits, rap music, cellular phones and vacations in Tuscany. Needs are genuine and come from within, and wants come from without. On closer inspection the difference between needs and wants is in the eye of the beholder and does not stand up to much scrutiny. In Galbraith's world even culture would be trivial. (But try telling children that they really don't need a video game.) In a world where we're mesmerized by advertisers and marketers, no-growthers see rampant consumerism, more useless gadgets, built-in product obsolescence and more pollution.

2   "Why Conventional Economics Spells Doom," *Toronto Star* (2 March 1991), p. D6.

3   The coal-burning locomotives that evoke strong nostalgia today were once considered by many to be "soot-belching contraptions" that were a blight on the landscape. Each generation has its own detestable technology.

4   Richard Lipsey, *Economic Growth: Science and Technology and Institutional Change in a Global Economy*, Publication No.4 (Toronto: Canadian Institute for Advanced Research, June 1991), p. 30.

5   Government of Canada, *Canada's Green Plan* (Ottawa: Supply and Services, 1990).

6   The Environmental Protection Agency (EPA) in the United States estimates that the cost of pollution control already in place will go from $100 billion today to $150 billion, in constant dollars, by the year 2000— or approximately 2.7 percent of the GNP. Most of this will go in cleaning up contaminated land sights. See William Reilly, "The Next Environmental Policy: Preventing Pollution," *Domestic Affairs*, summer 1991.

7   In global terms, Canada is a minor polluter. We produce only 2 percent of the world's CO_2, 2 percent of nitrous oxides, 2 percent of CFCs, and only 1 percent of the methane gas. This means we can't go it alone. We need the cooperation of all countries to reduce the gases that contribute to the earth's warming. See *Canada's Green Plan*.

8   Dr. Suzuki was highly critical of the Brundtland Report. He argued that the only solution to protecting the environment was no-growth and massive income distribution from developed to underdeveloped countries. If this were done, per capita income would be around $2,750 U.S. in 1985 dollars. A family of four would be below the poverty line in the United States and Canada. No one would accept such a Utopian proposal. The environment won't be better protected by making everyone poor. See Lipsey, "*Economic Growth.*"

MYTH 21

THE 'ROARING EIGHTIES' WERE GOOD ECONOMIC YEARS

Few decades have had the economic impact and ups and downs of the 1980s. It started with one of the worst economic downturns since the depression and ended with one of the strongest and longest periods of growth in modern times. In between we experienced a stock market crash and recovery, wide interest rates swings, record levels of inflation in the early 1980s, and real estate prices that made everyone lucky enough to own a home rich, on paper at least. Over the same period women changed the face of the work force by entering the labour market in record numbers, increasing their participation rates to 58 percent by 1987, the highest in the G7 nations. Over two million new jobs were created. It was the decade when the yuppie came into his or her own. They filled business schools looking for MBAs, while the heros of the day were junk bond traders and corporate raiders with names such as Boesky, Milken, Campeau and Trump. It was the age of money when anything was possible, and anyone could make a million. The 1980s were a time of dramatic economic change given all the construction, plant expansions and fast-paced technological change, and the promise of better things to come. It seemed the optimism and good times would go on forever.

We are all familiar with the big winners in the 1980s (and losers of the 1990s), but how did the average citizen and wage earner do? Were they swept up by the rising tide of expectations and wealth creation and left better off by the end of the decade? Unfortunately for most, they exited the decade no better off than they entered it. But the myth lingers that the 1980s were the best of economic times.

WHERE DID ALL THE MONEY GO?

The 1980s may have been good for some people, but not everybody. Statistics show that the average family income after taxes was $40,200 in 1980 but had only risen to $40,400 by 1989. That comes as a surprise to a lot of people who saw the 1980s as a time of prosperity, consumerism, and economic growth. It is true that we went through a lot of economic ups and downs, but in the end we were no further ahead than when we started.

In fact, the previous decades were better than the eighties. Over the 1970s the average family after-tax income grew by 22 percent. The previous decades were just as good. Family income increased by 34 percent in the 1960s and 27 percent in the 1950s.[1] In the early 1980s average income dropped 6 percent and only increased 8 percent from 1984 to 1989. One problem was taxes. They took a larger share of personal income in the latter half of the decade. Taxes went from 15 percent in 1980 to 19 percent by 1989 as the average take-home pay began to shrink. Even though people received more in government transfer payments through unemployment insurance and social assistance, taxes went up faster than government handouts. At the same time, the federal government instituted tax clawbacks of family allowances and old age pensions from high-income taxpayers. The decade was a time when the federal government was trying to handle high deficits with more taxes, while government fringe benefits, such as pensions, were being enriched.

What about income distribution? Were the rich getting richer, and the poor getting poorer during the 1980s? According to Statistics Canada, both groups stayed put throughout the decade in terms of income distribution. Even the middle-income groups made no ground during the 1980s, neither increasing nor decreasing their share of income.[2]

That is what occurred with average family incomes, but what about individual wages and salaries? One would think those had moved up with the perceived boom of the 1980s. But nothing of the kind happened, even with wages. Real wages, after taking inflation into account, peaked in 1976 and have stayed flat since then (see Figure 21.1). In fact wages actually shrunk in 1989 by 0.03 percent

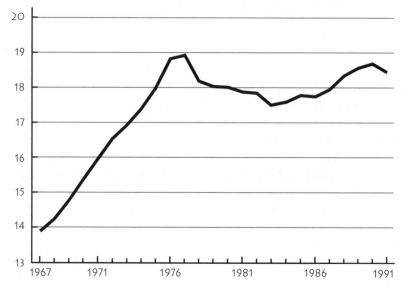

Source: StatsCan.

FIGURE 21.1   REAL WAGES DROPPED DURING THE 1980S

from their 1976 high.[3] If any one trait during the 1980s stands out, it is not so much what happened, but what did *not* happen. There was a lot of speculation that somehow the economy was being polarized in terms of income, and that the middle classes were shrinking while the gap between the rich and poor widened. Although researchers found some polarization on average wages over the 1980s, that certainly was not the case for family incomes. The main reason was that Canada's tax structure and social programs took money from the haves and gave it to the have-nots — at least to the extent that no class was better or worse off.

What the numbers don't show is that the work force at the extreme ends of the pay scale was growing, while the number of jobs at the middle-income levels was shrinking. Put another way, the economy was producing high-wage and low-wage jobs simultaneously. Statistics Canada dubbed this phenomenon the good jobs, bad jobs scenario.[4] On the basis of the distribution of income, the share of the work force in the lower one-third rose from 36.4 percent in 1967 to 39.4 percent in 1986, while the upper third increased by roughly the same proportion. The middle group dropped by 5.3 percent. The earnings of the lower group stayed at about 12.5 percent, but the upper group increased by 5.4 percent; obviously the exact amount was lost by the middle section of the labour force. Although there was little or no polarization in family income, that wasn't the case for earnings.

INCOMES DURING THE 1980S

What was going on? How could families in the middle- and lower-earnings levels continue to maintain their income while losing ground regarding their wages? The answer was simple. More women were going to work and increasing the number of two-income families in order to maintain their standard of living. By 1989, the number of two-income families increased to 62.3 percent from 30 percent in 1967.[5] The 1980s were a time of stagnant wage increases; more women entering the labour market; higher taxes and transfer payments, which stabilized family incomes; and growing jobs in the low- and high-earnings categories. In short, more and more people were working just to keep from losing ground. Although the 1980s appeared to be booming, it was mostly illusory in terms of rising incomes. Where were people finding jobs? There was a dramatic increase in the dynamic or high value jobs in business services such as engineers, consultants and architects, but traditional services that employed low-skilled workers, such as in restaurants and hotels, were also expanding.[6]

Almost 3.1 million Canadians, or roughly 23 percent of the labour force, worked in serving food, selling merchandise in retail stores, performing clerical work in service industries, cleaning hospitals, schools and offices, or providing some other form of personal service. These jobs accounted for much of the employment growth in the 1980s. Yet for the most part these are the jobs that are poorly paid, lead nowhere, and are at the bottom of the job ladder. These jobs were not being filled by teenagers and those just entering the labour market for the first time as was once thought, but by second-earners in families struggling to make ends meet. [7]

HOW TO STAY RICH

The key factor behind Canada's stagnant income growth was the dismal performance of productivity, that is, the amount of output produced by each worker. We can raise our standard of living, or increase how much we consume by one of three ways: first, by putting more people to work, such as by increasing the participation of women in the labour force; second, using our savings not for investment, but for consumption; or third, producing more output per worker. The first two solutions only work in the short term. We can add more workers to the labour force as we did in the latter part of the 1980s; however, there are limits to how many people can be put to work. The second is also a short-term solution because we can only live so long on our savings to maintain our standard of living before all savings are exhausted. In other words, you can eat all the grain this year, but there won't be any for planting in the future. The only long-term solution is improving productivity per worker. If we produce more, we can consume more. Our ability to increase our standard of living ultimately depends on how productive we are.[8]

How have we done over the 1980s? The answer is, not well. Labour productivity growth measured by total output per hour worked averaged about one percent from 1976 to 1989. In the 1950s productivity growth averaged 4 percent and 4.3 percent in the 1960s. It maintained that pace in the early 1970s, but dropped quickly after that. Why? The jury is still out on that question. But whatever the reason, our inability to increase output is directly tied to our falling standard of living and declining wages.[9] In the 1960s and 1970s, real wages (after inflation), increased over 3 percent each year. Over the late 1970s and entire 1980s real wages actually declined by 0.3 percent mainly because productivity growth was at historical lows. If labour productivity growth in the 1980s had been the same as in the previous two decades, our standard of living would be about 50 percent higher today. That's how important productivity is to the economy.

For all the sound and fury of the 1980s, economically speaking, they were a failure. Fortunes were made and lost, the economy went through wild swings from recessions to booms, and more jobs were created and lost in a shorter amount of time than in any other period in Canadian history. In the end our inability to structure our economy to invest and become more productive meant that we had little to show for a decade of extremes. In economics there's no free lunch. You can't consume what you don't produce for very long.

NOTES

1. Roger Love and Susan Poulin, "Family income and inequality in the 1980s," *Perspectives*, Statistics Canada, autumn 1991. The authors find the same results even when they measure median income over the 1980s. That is, the median income level where 50 percent of the families earn more, and 50 percent of the families earn less. Over the decade, median family income followed the general pattern shown by mean family income. In fact, the median income in 1989 was less ($36,800) than in 1980 ($37,300), which means there were larger changes for higher-income families.

2. The technique used by Statistics Canada to estimate income distribution is to segment or break down families into ten income categories, from a low of $11,600 to a high of $88,800. At the beginning of the decade, the lowest group received 2.5 percent of total income compared with 21.7 percent for the highest or richest group. By 1989, the lowest group received 2.9 percent and the highest group 22 percent.

3. Wages, measured in 1989 dollars, were around $14.50 an hour in 1976. By the mid 1980s they dipped below $14.00 and settled at $14.25 by 1989.

4. Statistics Canada measures this by taking the work share given seven categories of income levels. All the work share gains between 1967 and 1986 took place at the very extremes of the distribution among individuals earning either less than 50 percent or more than 150 percent of the median.

5. "Report on Canada" *The Globe and Mail* (25 October 1991).

6. Jobs in the goods and service industries grew at an average annual rate of 2.5 percent from 1967 to 1986. Personal services grew at a rate of 3.8 percent over that time period, and business services at 7.3 percent. See Economic Council of Canada, *Good Jobs, Bad Jobs, Employment in the Service Economy* (Ottawa: Supply and Services, 1990).

7. The same trends are occurring in the U.S. economy but on a grander scale. One estimate puts the number of dead-end jobs at about 42 percent of their labour force, or 45 million workers, dominated by the traditional service sectors such as restaurants and hotels. This same study pessimistically predicts that by the year 2000, 70 percent of the jobs will be in this sector, and the rest in skilled labour. See Leonard A. Schlesinger and James L. Heskett, "The Service-Driven Service Company," *Harvard Business Review*, September–October 1991.

8. We can't ignore the fact that wages in the 1980s also dropped because of the declining influence of labour unions which represented a smaller share of the work force. Because of higher unemployment in the 1980s, workers were willing to make pay concessions to get more job security.

9. One reason labour productivity growth declined was due to an increase in the supply of labour as baby boomers came onto the market. More labour means lower wages as labour was more plentiful relative to capital. This labour force was not only younger but less experienced, which may have contributed to lower labour productivity growth rates.

INFLATION IS HERE TO STAY
BECAUSE PRICES ALWAYS
GO UP

ontrary to popular belief, prices don't always go up. Price stability has been the rule and not the exception throughout history. In Canada, prices only started rising in the late 1940s (see Figure 22.1). Since Confederation prices were generally stable until the Second World War.[1] What acclimatized us to higher inflation was our recent bout with double digit inflation over the late 1970s and early 1980s; and because of it, we believed inflation just wouldn't end.

Since those high-inflation years, however, prices have dropped dramatically, and it looks as if they will stay down for awhile. By the spring of 1992 inflation was no higher than 1.6 percent, and in some months we have experienced deflation as the rate of price increases actually dropped below zero, something that has not happened in thirty years. We may be entering a long period of price stability, something unfamiliar to us in the last two decades.

If that is the case, why do we persist in believing that inflation is a permanent feature of economic life when in fact double-digit inflation is the exception rather than the rule? Part of the problem is that few understand what inflation is and how it's measured. A second factor is conditioning. In this the media has to take some responsibility. We hear over and over how the cost of living is always going up, and how fifty years ago a dollar could buy someone a movie, a meal and transportation home. We are reminded how a shopping cart of groceries that cost $100 in 1991, cost only $17 in 1950. The idea we are being given is that we get less for more. But the media neglects to remind us that wages have not stood still either. In 1950 the average wage was $1.04 per hour, while today it is over $13. However, the impression that sticks is that the dollar is continuously eroding along with our incomes. Since 1940 real per capita incomes have gone from around $6,000 to over $20,000 in 1990. Since 1870, real incomes (after inflation)

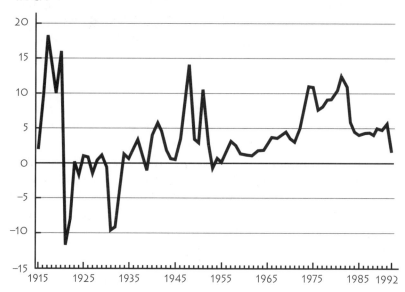

PERCENT
CHANGE
IN CPI

Source: StatsCan.

FIGURE 22.1   PRICES DO NOT ALWAYS GO UP

have gone up twelvefold.[2] We nostalgically look back on the days of a strong currency. What we really lament is that we can not have 1950 prices and 1990 incomes.[3]

THE CPI: WHAT IT DOES AND DOES NOT DO

To understand the misperceptions, it is important to understand the definition of inflation. Inflation is a persistent rise in prices over an extended period of time. It's not a one-shot increase in prices. If prices went up 10 percent last year and only 5 percent this year, the *rate* of inflation has dropped 50 percent, even though prices are still higher from one year to the other. If in the third year the rate of change is zero, then there's no inflation at all. For inflation to exist, the rate of change has to be positive month over month, or year over year. That is what people mean when they talk of an increase in the cost of living.

The most common measurement of the cost of living is the Consumer Price Index (CPI), which tracks the changes in household goods. There is no such thing as a cost of living index, or at least not of the kind we think of as an index. The CPI is calculated by tracking the average change in prices of a basket of goods and services that consumers buy. It is an average of the changes in the prices of all goods. If consumers spend 25 percent of their income on food, then the average is weighted to reflect the importance of that commodity. The basket contains about 490 products ranging from food, haircuts, housing costs, clothing, medical care, movie tickets, and transportation. This basket is periodically updated to reflect consumer buying patterns. Each month Statistics Canada sends out an army of investigators to sixty-four cities to check how these prices have changed.[4] In a sense we all have a different inflation rate depending on the basket of goods we buy. Although the CPI is the most commonly used measure of cost of living, it remains an imperfect measure of price changes.

To begin with, the CPI by its nature overstates inflation in a number of ways. First, individuals change their buying patterns based on changing tastes. What's popular today may not be desirable tomorrow. For example, as we become more aware of our health, we change our buying patterns and cut back on red meats faster than Statistics Canada's ability to keep up with the changes. Second, people react not only to absolute price changes, but relative prices as well. If the price of butter goes up, less is bought while we look for less-costly substitutes. Even if butter prices remain the same and the cost of margarine falls, the relative price shift makes butter more expensive and we consume less of it; but the CPI still assumes we spend the same proportion of our income on butter. In this respect, the CPI is biased upwards. Third, the CPI does not take into consideration improvements in the quality of products. Computers are a good example. Equipment that would have cost you $5,000 a few years ago costs less than $1,000 today. Consumers don't spend less, they just buy dramatically more powerful machines.

OTHER MEASURES OF INFLATION

The CPI is not the only measure of prices. Statistics Canada also keeps close watch on domestic manufactured goods with both the

Industrial Product Price Index (IPPI), and the Raw Material Price Index (RMPI). The IPPI follows prices charged by Canadian manufacturers, while the RMPI monitors prices of raw material inputs sold in Canada. There is one more index, known as the GDP deflator, which measures the average price of *all* goods and services in the economy. These three indicators routinely show inflation rates lower than the CPI because they cover a broader range of goods.

If we know that the CPI tends to overstate inflation, and there are indicators that are more broadly based, why not revise or get rid of it? The reasons that we don't are both practical and political. Although the CPI is imperfect, it comes closest to measuring the rise in the cost of living of the average citizen. Other indices that measure price movements for wholesale or industrial products do not come close to measuring what consumers really buy. It is consumer prices, including imports, that we want to measure. Politically, organized labour probably would not go along with the idea of revising the CPI because they benefit from a higher reported inflation rate when setting wage demands. Any downward changes in prices would also make cost of living allowances less lucrative.

WHAT IS WRONG WITH INFLATION?

In 1988 the governor of the Bank of Canada, John Crow, made it clear he wanted zero-inflation. Haunted by the high prices of the decade, the Bank of Canada had resolved to eliminate inflation from the Canadian landscape. Zero-inflation tolerance was the goal. However, we must ask the question, what's wrong with inflation? In Canada the elderly and others on fixed incomes are protected from the effects of inflation because their incomes and old age security payments are indexed to the cost of living.[5] It is true that a quarter cannot buy a coffee today when it once bought an entire meal; but if a dinner takes a *smaller* bite of our average budget today than it once did, what is the problem? In that sense nominal prices (before inflation) are up, but real prices (after inflation) are down — and it's real prices we should be worried about. However, it's not that simple. Inflation has more subtle and profound costs that may not be apparent at first glance.

Consumers, as a group, make millions of decisions each day about what to buy and how much to spend based on many factors; but as already mentioned, one of the most important is prices, both relative and absolute. That is how producers get their signals about what to produce. Now imagine what happens when prices are distorted by rapid inflation. It's like jamming a radio signal — when there's too much interference we find it hard to discern the signal — we can't tell anymore what's expensive and what's not. Consumers start making bad buying decisions, which result in enormous losses known as "allocative inefficiencies."[6] Time and effort are also wasted in just keeping up with price changes. Think of the catastrophic productive waste in a country like Russia after the fall of the Soviet Union where prices of many commodities shot up 300 and 400 percent overnight after government subsidies were removed. The economy not only suffered massive efficiency losses, but consumers were under added psychological stress and anxiety as they saw their life savings evaporate. In periods of runaway inflation, people are busier spending (and waiting in line) in an effort to buy before prices get even higher, making the inflation cycle even worse. Sooner or later the entire monetary system breaks down and people revert to bartering.

The constant theme in public policy is: where there are losers you are sure to find winners, even during times of inflation. When prices rise without warning, debtors win out over lenders as debts are paid back with less expensive dollars.[7] One of the biggest winners when unanticipated prices go up are governments. In the past they have only too well understood this rule, which partly accounts for their reluctance to fight inflation too strenuously.[8] One way governments win is through "tax creep." Because our income tax system is essentially progressive, the higher the income, the higher the marginal rate of tax. Inflation pushes people into higher marginal tax brackets without increases in their real income. Since 1975, taxpayers demanded to be protected from higher taxes by indexing the tax system to inflation. Inflation itself no longer pushes people into higher tax brackets unless real income goes up. The irony with indexation is that during times of high price increases, it perpetuates and virtually institutionalizes inflation into the system: the very problem it was designed to protect us against. It treats the symptoms and not the causes of the problem.

WHO IS TO BLAME?

Inflation was once described as being like a crowd at a football game. If everyone sits down everyone gets to see the game. But as soon as one fan stands to get a better view, everyone else starts standing and no one's view is any better. An individual or group can improve their position in the economy by bargaining for higher wages or by increasing their prices. These people do win, but only at the expense of others. When these higher costs are passed along, everyone starts standing, and no one is willing to sit down first unless forced by government action.[9]

In a nutshell that is what happens with inflation. The phenomenon of inflation is partly psychological as well as economic. Although the roots of price increases are economic in nature, what helps drive inflation is people's behaviour. If we believe prices will go up in the future, then we build that expectation into our present price and wage demands. In the end it becomes a self-fulfilling prophecy. When that mind-set takes hold, we see prices going in only one direction, and that is up.

The football analogy above helps us understand what happens after inflation takes hold, but how it gets started is more problematical. One theory blames the unions for initiating unreasonable wage demands, which forces business to pass along higher prices in order to maintain their level of profits. This notion is referred to in economics texts as cost-push. Another theory is know as demand-pull,[10] which blames governments for stimulating too much activity in the economy by overspending or undertaxing. Both situations can only produce sustained inflation with the agreement of the consumer who is more than willing to pay the higher prices. If consumers were a little more discerning or price sensitive, inflation would not last for long. But no one's willing to "sit down first."

Another theory puts the blame squarely at the feet of monetary authorities who put too much money into the system. Some economists believe that what starts the ball rolling is irrelevant, but claim that what keeps it going is an increase in money supply. When the growth in money supply increases faster than the economy's ability to produce more goods and services, something has to give: result, inflation. To a monetarist, if a government wants to avoid higher prices then it should make sure that the money supply grows no faster than the rate of growth in the national economy.

Do taxes fuel more inflation? Yes and no. Taxes, especially those that affect consumer prices (for example, the GST adds to the price of goods and services), inevitably force the CPI upwards. But if you remember our definition of inflation, taxes are a one-shot increase in prices. When the GST was introduced on January 1, 1991, the CPI jumped 2.4 percent that month. At that rate inflation would have been over 28 percent for the year. The CPI quickly settled down the following month to an annual rate of 5 percent. In fact, 1991 saw one of the lowest rate increases since the 1960s. The GST is not inflationary in the long run. Critics will have to find another argument against it if they don't like the tax.[11]

Governments try to rid themselves of inflation but, unfortunately, the attempts come at a cost. To fight the high prices in the early 1980s, the federal government so tightened the supply of money that it sent interest rates into double digits and started one of the worst recessions since the 1930s. The "medicine" worked but it almost killed the patient. It had to be strong enough to convince people that double-digit price increases were not a permanent part of our economic landscape. The psychology of higher prices had to be broken. As borrowing became tougher, consumers and businesses cut back borrowing and investing. The result was lower demand and lower prices, but with an unemployment rate of over 13 percent. Prices came down but at an enormous cost to society. The government vowed never to let inflation get so out of hand, which explains in part why the Bank of Canada is so vigilant today.

The problem now is that governments might be fighting inflation too energetically. If inflation is bad, deflation may be worse. It's a sign of economic inactivity and weakness. Economic crises not only happen when prices get out of hand, but also when prices collapse as they did during the depression of the 1930s. We then had price stability, but little else. It is a constant reminder that prices do not move in just one direction.

NOTES

1   The same price stability also occurred in Britain and the United States. For Britain, prices before 1933 fell more than they increased going all the way back to 1661. In the United States prices usually fell from 1820, when data was collected, up until the early 1930s. See *The Economist* (22 February 1992), p. 68.

2   See Economic Council of Canada, *A Joint Venture* (Ottawa: Supply and Services, 1991).

3   People live in a world of money illusion. Suppose you give someone a $100 raise and inflation was 60 percent, leaving a real increase of only $40. Now offer that same person $40 with steady prices. Lester Thurow found that most people prefer the second alternative even though both cases are identical. Why? Because in the first instance people see the entire $100 as theirs and inflation has robbed them of most of it. See Lester Thurow, *The Zero-Sum Society* (New York: Basic Books, 1980).

4   The rate of inflation is calculated as follows:

This year's price level – Last year's price level / Last year's price level × 100

5   Another group of winners during inflationary periods are the rich or those who can shift out of money into hard assets, such as real estate, art and precious metals. Those who managed to shift their wealth out of currency or low interest bearing accounts to hard assets end up winning big, as the price of these assets rise faster than the rate of inflation.

6   For example, if there's a shortage of a specific good because of an increase in demand, then the price of that good goes up. In an economy where prices are stable, producers supply more of the product in short supply because profits are to be made. The price system has done its job in properly identifying where producers should put their investments. But if prices are distorted because of inflation, producers have a tougher time knowing where to put their money and society's resources, leading to economic waste and inefficient allocation of resources.

7   But in time lenders learn to adjust by demanding higher interest to compensate them for anticipated future inflation.

8   A strong argument can be made that inflation, which reduces real transfers to individuals, is a deliberate policy of the federal government because not all programs are fully indexed. See David Johnson, "An Evaluation of the Bank of Canada's Zero Inflation Target: Do Michael Wilson and John Crow Agree?," *Canadian Public Policy*, September 1990.

9   This situation is often called the "tragedy of the commons." What's logical for one person becomes illogical if everyone does it.

10   There are also all the price increases that originate outside the country, such as OPEC raising the price of oil, or of any products that Canada imports. These "exogenous" price shocks also fall under the heading of cost-push inflation.

11   There is some evidence that the GST actually helped prices come down. The reason is that the tax replaced the 13 percent manufacturing sales tax, which affected the cost of manufactured goods in Canada. Now everything is taxed at 7 percent. The cost of services and consumer goods went up, but the cost of producing machinery and equipment dropped bringing down the overall cost of production, which eventually means lower prices for consumers. (By the third quarter of 1991, consumer prices were 5.2 percent higher than a year before while machinery and equipment prices were 8.3 percent lower. See Greg Ip, "Reviled GST May Be Delivering the Goods," *The Financial Post*, 10 January 1992.)

THE COST OF SEPARATION WILL BE MANAGEABLE FOR QUEBEC AND THE REST OF CANADA

What happens if Quebec separates, or Canada devolves more power to the provinces in an effort to keep the country together? What are the economic costs to Quebec and the rest of the country? This chapter doesn't deal so much with a myth about the economy as with a misunderstanding of economic costs for both Quebec and the rest of Canada if Quebec decides to leave Confederation or if Canada forms a looser federation.

Those who favour Quebec independence, or some form of sovereignty association, have a stake in minimizing the costs to both Quebec and Canada. A number of French Canadian economists and the leader of the Parti Québécois, Jacques Parizeau, assume that English Canada will bargain in good faith because it will be in its self-interest to do so. The feeling is that negotiations will be tough, but cool heads will prevail and the costs of adjustment to the split up of the country will be low. Those who believe in a strong central government make the opposite case: they feel that if Quebec decides to leave, "all bets are off" and forecast that the negotiations will be not only tough but also acrimonious. Under those circumstances the costs in terms of lost lower income, less investment, and higher unemployment could drive the costs of separation sky high for the rest of Canada, and especially for Quebec. This fundamental difference gives the overall impression that economists' opinions are widely scattered on the issue of the economic costs of Quebec separation. The projected costs have varied from a high of 10 percent of GDP estimated by the Fraser Institute to a low of 1.4 percent of GDP estimated by the Economic Council of Canada. It is important to note, however, that the differences of opinion are not based in disagreements on the technical and purely economic questions, but rather in the political scenarios of separation. That's why we cannot know the real costs.

Over the past few years there has been considerable work done on the economic impacts of Quebec independence. The three general observations about these studies are that, first, the costs of the break up of the country will be greater the more decentralized the country becomes; second, the economic impact would be greater for Quebec than the rest of Canada; and third, that no one knows what the exact costs of separation will be because until it happens, no one knows the conditions under which the country will be divided.

THE CASE FOR SOVEREIGNTY ASSOCIATION: THE LOW-COST SCENARIO

The most optimistic forecasts of the impact of Quebec sovereignty came mainly from French Canadian economists in their briefs before the Bélanger–Campeau Commission, which dealt with Quebec's constitutional and political future under Premier Robert Bourassa in 1991. The studies that dealt with the economics of Quebec's independence arrive at two basic conclusions: that the transitional costs involved in any separation would be minimal if the federal and Quebec governments negotiate rationally, and that the long-term costs would be low or negligible in terms of lost jobs, and a change in standard of living. To reach these conclusions, the Belanger–Campeau Commission made a number of crucial assumptions. First, that the trade relations with the rest of Canada and the United States would remain unchanged. This means that Canada would agree to a common market with Quebec in which they would behave much like the European Economic Community. They would reduce barriers between the regions of Canada, but maintain common tariff and nontariff barriers with other countries. Upon separation the United States would automatically sign a free trade agreement with Quebec similar to the one that now exists between Canada and the United States, and Quebec would quickly become a member of GATT.

The second assumption deals with monetary policy. Here the commission assumes that Quebec would have a common monetary policy with the rest of Canada by adopting the Canadian dollar as the common currency. Jacques Parizeau has said often that an independent Quebec could take the Canadian dollar as its currency without Ottawa's permission or endorsement. A third assumption is that Quebec's budgetary position would change little after the formation of a new state. The secretariat to the Bélanger–Campeau

Commission makes the argument that Quebec should assume only 18.5 percent of the national debt rather than its share based on population, which would be around 25 percent.[1] On the issue of loss of equalization payments to Quebec from the rest of Canada, the sovereigntists argue that Quebec would lose little if anything after separation, given that Quebec's tax contribution to Canada (so say Quebec's nationalists), are the same as the transfers from Ottawa.

A study done by the Economic Council of Canada[2] estimated that under the conditions of sovereignty association in which the federal government cuts out all buying from Quebec and the province no longer collects equalization payments, the loss to Quebec would be a drop in welfare equal to between 1.4 and 3.5 percent of its GDP.[3] Quebec nationalists jumped on these numbers to show that the costs would be low for Quebec and practically nonexistent for the rest of Canada. But the council's findings only showed what would happen if the federal government removed taxes and transfers and ignored the political consequences of splitting up the country. The picture changes considerably if international and national considerations are taken into account.

WILL THE REST OF CANADA GO ALONG? THE HIGH-COST SCENARIO

Internationally any political instability implies uncertainty, which means higher interest rates for international borrowing and less foreign investment. Although these things are hard to measure, some have tried. One study estimates that if international lenders charge 1 percent more to Canadian borrowers, the loss will slow growth in Canada's GDP equivalent to $8.6 billion (1986 dollars) over a ten-year period. Along with a higher borrowing rate facing governments, Canada can also expect less direct international investment. Lower investment of $1 billion dollars each year for ten years means 1 percent less capital and machinery to work with a 0.5 percent drop in productivity and real wages. We may not have to wait for separation in order to be affected by higher interest rates and less investment. International investors know the political climate in Canada and may already be charging a premium to invest here.[4]

Concerning the assumptions that after independence Quebec will sign on as a member of GATT and that the United States will extend the free trade agreement to Quebec, most experts agree that

Quebec will have little problem becoming a member of GATT, but that joining the Canada–U.S. free trade agreement, or NAFTA, is another matter. A "sovereign Quebec" will be negotiating with a "sovereign Canada," which means that Quebec will have to give up its industrial subsidies, forfeit protection of its financial institutions (i.e., the caisses populaires), open up its purchasing by government departments, stop Hydro-Quebec from subsidizing local industries, and get rid of existing barriers against goods and services from other provinces. Those who remember how difficult it was to negotiate the free trade agreement with the United States should know that Quebec's negotiations with Canada and the United States will be no easy matter. Quebec was allowed to keep a number of its protective programs because of its subnational status within Confederation; that won't be the case once it becomes a sovereign nation. In any event, Quebec would have to renegotiate entry into the Canada–U.S. free trade agreement and that means less protection than they have now. As trade expert Gordon Ritchie said, " if it were easy to agree on free trade, it would not have taken us 50 years to get tariffs down to present levels."[5] Here the rest of Canada would be in a better bargaining position than an independent Quebec. Canada ships only 6.8 percent of all manufacturing output to Quebec, while Quebec in turn exports over 26 percent to the rest of Canada.[6]

In terms of the idea of a new customs union between an independent Quebec and Canada, it's hard to see the rest of the country willing to pay higher tariffs to protect the textile, clothing, and furniture industries in Quebec. Continuing to protect these sectors is important to Quebec because these "soft" industries are located mainly in Quebec and account for about 48.5 percent of total Canadian employment in those industries. Quebec now has a surplus of $3.3 billion in these industries.[7] There would be a growing temptation to buy these products from lower-cost producers around the world, such as those in the Far East and South America. The same principle applies to agricultural products. Quebec dairy producers supply almost 50 percent of Canada's industrial milk at inflated prices protected by marketing boards — direct and indirect federal subsidies to Quebec, including protection under supply management schemes, amounted to $900 million in 1989. If Quebec dairy farmers had to sell their products at U.S. prices to the rest of Canada, they would stand to lose as much as $200 million annually. Some Quebec farm organizations have already advocated that existing supply management arrangements remain, arguing that they have a right to continue exporting agricultural products to other provinces as part of their "historical market." There is no chance this would ever be accepted by the rest of Canada.[8]

When it comes to the national debt and the Canadian dollar, things get more complicated. It would be naive to think the rest of Canada would go along with some of the conditions for sovereignty association put forth by Quebec nationalists. It is hard to see Quebec assuming only 18.5 percent of the national debt. This percentage is based on Quebec's share of total federal assets (buildings, Crown corporations, and the like); but since the debt was not incurred to purchase assets, there is no reason to split the debt on that basis. In fact, the higher national debt was partly incurred to pay higher unemployment insurance and transfer payments to Quebec. The Bélanger–Campeau Commission estimated Quebec receives a net fiscal gain of $409 per capita, or $2.7 billion from the federal government. A closer estimate would be based on population share at 25.5 percent, or the amount of debt incurred by the federal government on behalf of each region in the country, which would bring Quebec's portion to 30.9 percent.[9] This throws out any reasonable projections Quebec has about a manageable debt load, which would also increase the cost of borrowing internationally for an independent Quebec.[10]

Finally there is an assumption that Quebec will use the Canadian dollar as its official currency. According to some monetary authorities, the best option for both Quebec and the rest of the country after separation would be to continue with the status quo: a common currency with Quebec sitting on the board of the Bank of Canada. It is believed that this option is preferable to Quebec issuing its own currency — it would minimize costs all around and reassure the international financial community.[11] But a common currency presents serious risks to the rest of Canada. What happens, for example if a large Quebec financial institution goes bankrupt? If Quebec continues using the Canadian dollar as legal tender without permission, what does this mean for monetary policy in Canada? It is ironic that Quebec would chose this option, as the Parti Québécois insists it will, when they in effect will have no say over monetary policy, one of the most important levers of economic control. Quebec may end up having less economic independence than it has now if it allows the rest of Canada to unilaterally determine interest rates, money supply and ultimately prices, output and employment. Quebec may have freedom, but without independence.[12]

THE LIMITS OF ANALYSIS

It should be clear that trying to measure the costs of the break up of Canada is virtually impossible. There are simply too many factors to take into consideration. One imponderable is land. Will Quebec be able to walk away with the area now under its jurisdiction? The Cree and the rest of Canada may lay claim to Northern Quebec and James Bay, which was ceded to Quebec in 1912 on the understanding it would remain part of the country. That puts into dispute almost two-thirds of Quebec's approximately 1.5 million square kilometres of territory. Then there are the rights of non-Francophone Quebeckers. Would they be entitled to remain in Canada and separate from Quebec? It's impossible to know where the process would stop.

What is known is that any fragmentation of the Canadian economy erodes the gains from economic integration. These don't simply include the benefits of producing for a larger market and reaping the benefits of "economies of scale," one of the more important reasons Canada signed a trade deal with the United States.[13] Information and technology would not flow as smoothly between regions if Canada were to split up into different regions. People might not be able to work where they want to, nor would companies be able to go where they would earn the greatest profits. There is also the cost of uncertainty about Canada's future. Until that is resolved, Canadians will continue to pay higher interest rates from mortgages to business loans as foreign money lenders demand higher rates of return to offset the added risks of investing in a politically unsettled country.[14] All of these factors would have an effect on how efficiently the entire country operates. Any impediment to the movement of money, people and resources would in the end make us all poorer.[15] Those are the real hidden costs to the rest of Canada if the country should become more decentralized.

NOTES

¹ Based on that assumption, Quebec's overall debt would increase from 26.4 percent of its GDP to 63.9 percent, just below Canada's debt to GDP ratio. This would leave Quebec's debt to GDP position comparable to that of other European nations. See Patrick Grady, *The Economic Consequences of Quebec Sovereignty* (Vancouver: the Frazer Institute, 1991) p. 43.

² The Economic Council of Canada, *A Joint Venture: The Economics of Constitutional Options* (Ottawa: Supply and Services, 1991).

³ Small as a 3.5 percent decrease in GDP may seem, it translates into a drop in income of $1,800 per year for each family for an entire generation! See *The Financial Post*, (18 November 1991), p. 16.

⁴ Peter Dungan and Francois Vaillancourt, *Economic Impacts of Constitutional Reform: Modelling Some Pieces of the Puzzle*, policy study no. 91-8 (Toronto: University of Toronto press, 1991).

⁵ Gordon Ritchie, "Putting Humpty Dumpty Together Again," John McCallum (ed.), *Broken Links: Trade Relations After a Quebec Secession* (C.D. Howe Institute, October 1991), p. 18.

⁶ Grady, *The Economic Consequences of Quebec Sovereignty*, pp. 111–12.

⁷ These sectors also rely heavily on exports to the rest of Canada. For textiles, Quebec exports 51.7 percent to other provinces; 45 percent of clothing; and about 38 percent of furniture and fixtures. See Grady, *The Economic Consequences of Quebec Sovereignty*.

⁸ W.H. Furtan and R.S. Gray, "Agriculture in an Independent Quebec, " *Broken Links*, pp. 50–51.

⁹ Economic Council of Canada, *A Joint Venture*, p. 87.

¹⁰ If Quebec assumes 23.4 percent of the national debt, proportional to its share of Canada's GDP, Quebec's debt as a share of GDP will be about 96 percent, well above the 63.9 percent estimated when Quebec assumed only 18.5 percent of the national debt. This will make it more expensive for Quebec to attract the necessary foreign investment they will need as an independent nation.

¹¹ David E.W. Laidler and William B.P. Robson, *Two Nations, One Money? Canada's Monetary System Following a Quebec Secession* (C.D Howe Institute, September 1991). The second best option would be for Quebec to use the Canadian dollar without any influence over monetary policy. The worst option would be for Quebec to issue its own currency floating against the Canadian or U.S. currency. The option of a Quebec currency fixed to the Canadian or U.S. dollar didn't fare any better. The French Canadian economist Bernard Fortin estimates that a separate currency could cost $40 billion.

¹² The losses for Quebec don't end here. Quebeckers would bear the costs of higher telephone rates, and higher bilingualism costs covering labelling and documentation now covered by the federal government. Who controls the shipping routes through the St. Lawrence would also be in question. Quebeckers would also risk losing about 25,000 jobs in the federal government of those employed mainly in the Hull-Ottawa area. More Anglophones and corporations could also move out of Quebec in the event of separation, taking even more needed talent with them. For more information, see Patrick Grady, *The Economic Consequences of Québec Sovereignty*.

13 A loss in the benefits of economies of scale could translate into lower capital and labour productivity. One study put this potential loss in total factor productivity at 2 percent in GDP over ten years. See Dungan and Vaillancourt, *Economic Impacts of Constitutional Reform.*

14 One can make the argument that we are already paying higher interest rates in Canada because of the higher premium demanded by those investing in Canada and buying government bonds (given the uncertainty of separation), or the fact that a looser federation may mean a less-efficient, and therefore, less profitable country.

15 Peter Brimelow writing in *Forbes*, 2 March 1992, argues that GDP per capita for the rest of Canada would actually rise if Quebec left Confederation because it is a drag, on the whole, through transfer payments. This ignores the dynamic, but immeasurable, gains Quebec and the rest of Canada enjoy as an integrated economy.

THE U.S. ECONOMY IS IN
DECLINE

The American dream seems on the verge of collapse. It is faced with the intractable social problems of drugs, crime, illiteracy, AIDS, homelessness, and a health care system that is the most expensive in the world (yet 30 million people in the United States have no health protection whatever). On the economic front, things look just as bad.

The last decade saw the stock market crash, a borrowing and consumption binge that turned the United States into the world's largest debtor nation, massive deficits, declining savings and productivity rates, a crumbling infrastructure and a steady erosion in the standard of living of the middle class. No institution seemed invulnerable when General Motors and IBM were shedding tens of thousands of jobs, losing market share at alarming rates, and posting massive losses. Critics can be forgiven for thinking that it was the beginning of the end for American economic dominance. It seemed America was collapsing and becoming a second-class economic power, following the same route as Britain at the turn of the last century. It appeared only a matter of time before the United States gave way to stronger Japanese and European economic powers. This pessimism was fuelled by a steady stream of books and articles documenting America's economic malaise.[1] Many of us in Canada wondered whether we would be taken down into the vortex of the U.S. decline.[2]

We know that the United States faces daunting social problems, but are the rumours of imminent collapse of its economy true? The answer is that most of the arguments about the decline of the American economy are products of wishful thinking rather than hard evidence. The declinists' main arguments centre around three major trends: growing trade and budget deficits, eroding global economic power, and a slowdown in R&D investment coupled with a deteriorating educational system.[3] It's important to look at each of these.

Mounting Budget and Trade Deficits

Few indicators are as alarming as America's rising trade and budget deficits over the last decade — to many, it is a sure sign that Americans are living on debt and borrowed time. Over a few short years the United States went from the world's largest lender to the biggest debtor nation. By 1987 it owed over $400 billion U.S. to other countries, while assets owned by foreigners, such as the British and Japanese, doubled. At the same time, the U.S. government was running up record budget deficits; in 1992, it was $400 billion. To make matters worse, Americans owed nearly half of this new debt to foreign lenders. It seemed America was addicted to foreign money. To many the day of reckoning was soon to be at hand when these debts would have to be repaid.[4]

What happened to put the U.S. economy in such a vulnerable situation? Declinists saw a fundamental weakening in the economy where Americans were losing their ability to compete and were interested more in buying and consuming than in saving and investing. The perception is that the United States went on an unprecedented spending spree during the 1980s that was financed by the savings of others, such as the Japanese and Germans, who were more than willing to lend their excess savings abroad at high interest rates. Pessimists say that as soon as foreign lenders see how weak the U.S. economy really is and interest rates start rising in their own countries, they will call in their loans and the United States will be plunged into an abyss. However, that's only one interpretation, and a wrong one at that.

Growing deficits, the difference between tax revenues and expenditures, were not caused by structural problems in the economy, but were the result of Reagan's policies of the early 1980s: lower taxes, more military spending, and a strong dollar. When taxes were lowered, consumers did not work more and invest more as was predicted (see Myth 14), but spent more, especially the rich. Low savings and higher spending meant Americans bought more Japanese electronics and European vacations. The result was a negative current account balance.[5] Because the U.S. government was not cutting back on spending, it financed the deficit with foreign borrowing by keeping interest rates high. This in turn kept the dollar strong, making imports cheaper and exports more expensive. In other words, the twin deficits, both trade and budget, are closely linked and reinforce each other. If that's the case, then, the deficits did not come from a weakening economy (although competitiveness did play a factor), but from Reagan's wrong-headed policy of lower taxes and high spending.

In other words, the United States has a transitional deficit rather than a structural deficit. That means that better policies can get rid of it. One way is to raise taxes. The average American family is undertaxed by international standards. For example, a family of four with an income of $80,000 a year are taxed at a marginal rate of 28 percent compared to 58 percent in Germany.[6] In fact, the current account deficit was all but gone by 1991 mainly because of rising exports.[7] But if services like consulting and air travel are added, the United States actually has a surplus.

Does the notoriety of being the world's biggest debtor bring other problems? Not really, because U.S. debts are not like those of Latin American countries. Foreign countries seem more than willing to lend the United States all the money it needs. If others want to invest in a country, it's a sign of that country's strength rather than weakness in that the investors expect a higher rate of return than in their own country.[8] Sony and BMW are lining up to invest in the United States. By the end of 1988, foreigners owned $1.8 trillion U.S. in assets. One worry is that the Japan has been "buying up" or "taking over" the United States, but according to the U.S. Department of Commerce, the largest investor is Britain, which holds twice the Amercian assets ($102 billion) of Japan ($53 billion), followed closely by the Netherlands. Best estimates put total U.S. wealth in the hands of foreigners at only 2 to 3 percent, and total land holdings between 0.5 percent to 1.0 percent. There is a worry that foreign investors may one day decided to pull out of the United States and go home. That would be hard to do since most of their assets are in factories, hotels and office buildings. If they did pull out, that would lower the value of the U.S. dollar and consequently the value of their own investments in the United States.[9]

Eroding Global Economic Power

One of the biggest myths about the U.S. economy is that it is losing its world manufacturing market share. It is true that the United States controlled 45 percent of total world output in the early 1950s, but that was after the war when America's industrial capacity was left intact. Today the U.S. share remains between 20 and 25 percent, the same since 1970. According to the U.S. Council on Competitiveness, the share of world exports has also held steady at around 12 percent. The United States still controls around 25 percent of the world's exports in high-technology products, a number unchanged since the mid 1960s.[10]

It seems the dreaded rumours of deindustrialization and the "hollowing out" of manufacturing are also exaggerated. Everything from cars to chemicals account for 23.3 percent of GNP, up from 20 percent in 1982. A U.S. Department of Commerce study in 1990 found not only that manufacturing was alive and well, but also that it was thriving and undergoing an industrial renaissance.[11] Manufacturing productivity grew at 3.6 percent over the 1980s, three times the levels from the 1970s. The Japanese industrial growth after World War II was so impressive mainly because they started from a lower base than the United States and Canada. Now that both countries are roughly at the same level of industrial sophistication, there's little reason why the Japanese economy should grow any faster.

A number of studies that compare international standards of living among nations use existing currency exchange rates. But these exchange rates do not take into consideration different price levels in various countries. For example, the average Japanese may have a higher salary when yens are converted to U.S. dollars, but rents in Tokyo are considerably higher than in Boston. The distortion is a bit like comparing your take-home pay today with ten years ago without taking inflation into consideration. Once these price differences are taken into account, the U.S. standard of living is the highest in the world. In making this adjustment economists use a term called purchasing power parity. Starting with the most basic measurement of wealth, per capita GDP, the average American is 17 percent ahead of Germany and 22 percent ahead of Japan. In fact the Japanese work about 260 hours more a year than Americans do in order to enjoy a lower standard of living. The real winners are the Germans who are able to enjoy their wealth by working 10 percent fewer hours than Americans. What allows the Americans to stay ahead of the Japanese? The answer is productivity. In some sectors of manufacturing, Japan and Germany are close to the United States. However, and this might come as a surprise to many, Japanese productivity is only about 74 percent of that of America's, while Germany is 78 percent. (See Figure 24.1.) Only Canada comes close to U.S. productivity levels. Japan is very efficient in the pro-

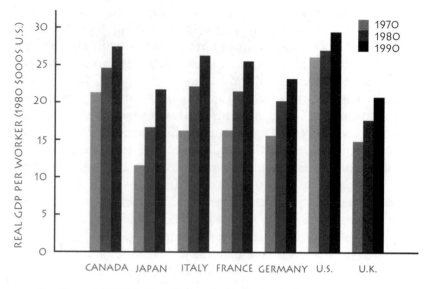

REAL GDP PER WORKER (1980 $000S U.S.)

■ 1970
■ 1980
■ 1990

CANADA JAPAN ITALY FRANCE GERMANY U.S. U.K.

Sources: StatsCan and OECD (adjusted by purchasing power parities)

FIGURE 24.1   U.S. WORKERS ARE STILL THE MOST PRODUCTIVE

duction of such things as VCRs and industrial and office equipment, but not enough to offset America's lead in pharmaceuticals, aircraft, textiles, construction materials and raw materials. Americans also have the most efficient service industries and the most productive agricultural sector.[12]

Declining Education

One major area in which the United States is clearly falling behind is education, especially from pre-school to grade 12. Even though Americans spend about as much per capita for education as other countries in the G-7 nations, students fail to perform at the level of students in Canada, Europe and Japan in the maths and sciences. Seventeen percent of American seventeen-year-olds are functionally illiterate. The United States is good at producing what Robert Reich of Harvard calls "symbolic analysts" (lawyers, consultants, engineers, scientists, architects, designers, writers, teachers, etc.) but not very good at the lower "routine production services." According to economist Lester Thurow of the Massachusetts Institute of Technology, success depends on educating the bottom

50 percent of the population if America hopes to be competitive. The Germans and Japanese concentrate on training workers on the shop floors while the United States invests in managers and professional employees.[13] Even though America has a poor elementary and secondary system, its universities and research facilities are the best in the world. If America is good at anything, it's good at ideas. In fact, the United States is a virtual "idea factory" leading the world by far in Nobel Prizes and scientific ideas.[14] Finally, even the Japanese admit that the United States remains ahead in high-tech industries. Of the 110 critical technologies in 1991, U.S. firms dominated in 43.[15]

IS THE UNITED STATES "DOWN AND OUT"?

Predicting the decline of the U.S. economy isn't new. This is at least the fifth time since the 1950s that pessimists have forecast the end of American economic dominance. The first scare came in 1958 when the Soviet Union became the first nation in space with the Sputnik. The late 1960s saw the second, with U.S. world power waning as they became mired in the Vietnam War, followed by the third with the OPEC oil embargo in 1973. The fourth declinist surge came in the late 1970s with a combination of set-backs including, at home, Watergate; and, internationally the expansion of Soviet power in Central America and Africa, ending with the Soviet invasion of Afghanistan. Now the United States is confronted with rising trade and budget deficits, and the competitive and financial threat from Japan.[16]

In any event, predicting the end of U.S. economic domination is a risky and highly speculative venture. Often in the debate about America's economic health, we tend to forget just how big and powerful that country is in absolute terms. The U.S. gross domestic product is almost three times that of Japan and four times greater than Germany's. The American work force is twice that of Japan's at 120 million. Since the economic expansion in 1982, the United States has added over 20 million to its work force alone or four times the number of jobs created over that same period in Japan, Germany, the United Kingdom, France and Italy.

Will this strength continue? That depends on a number of factors including how well the United States performs as global markets become more integrated. One positive sign is demographics. The U.S. population is beginning to mature as baby boomers reach their most productive years, similar to the age groupings in Germany and Japan. Now that the Cold War is over, the United States will not have to misallocate as large a share of its resources in nonproductive defence products. This should mean higher productivity, lower unemployment and higher savings. Nevertheless, it faces major social problems, a decaying infrastructure and a deteriorating educational system. But the American economic and political system is too open and competitive to be in decline for long. Some optimists go even further and argue that not only is the country not stagnating, but that it is on the verge of an unstoppable economic boom fuelled by wide-open markets and fast-paced technological innovations.[17] Even if nothing changes, America won't crumble overnight. Economist Paul Kruger has said that even in the worst case "there is nothing in the basic arithmetic of U.S. budget deficits, foreign debt, or inflation that would prevent [the United States] from continuing more or less with current policies for another decade."[18] This should not leave any illusions about what might happen in the future. Poor policies could still make the United States a second-rate power. But for all its problems, it still remains the preferred place on earth for immigrants from around the world. If America has any strength, it's the capacity to adapt to changing economic conditions.

NOTES

[1] A sample of the declinist writings were Paul Kennedy's *The Rise and Fall of the Great Powers: Economic Change and Military Conflict from 1500 to 2000* (New York: Random House, 1987); Peter G. Peterson's article entitled "The Morning After," *The Atlantic,* October 1987; and Robert Kuttner, "The Abyss," *The New Republic,* 29 October 1990.

[2] This was an argument of the Canadian nationalists who were opposed to the free trade agreement with the United States in 1987: "Why should Canada hitch its wagon to a falling star with an agreement that brings our economies closer together?" Some critics of the agreement, such as the writer Margaret Atwood, claimed that we would not get their markets, but instead would inherit their crime rate, health problems and gun laws: *Ottawa Citizen* (19 December 1987).

[3] Samuel P. Huntington, "The US — Decline or Renewal?", *Foreign Affairs,* winter 1988/89, p. 76.

[4] Benjamin Friedman, *Day of Reckoning* (New York: Vintage, 1989), p. 5.

[5] It's true Americans tend to save only 5 percent of disposable income compared with 15 percent for the Japanese; however, there isn't a need to save as much as long as others are willing to invest their savings in the U.S.

[6] Lester Thurow at MIT argues that a small increase in taxes would eliminate the budget deficit. See Charles C. Mann, "The Man With All the Answers," *The Atlantic* January 1990, p. 60.

[7] The U.S. current account deficit went from $143 billion in 1987 to $29 billion in 1991. See Alan S. Blinder, "Economic Viewpoint," *Business Week*, 6 April 1992, p. 12.

[8] Foreign ownership is fast becoming irrelevant as international companies go into joint ventures producing products where they can get the best deal. When Pontiac LeMans are made in Korea, and U.S. semiconductors are designed by Russian engineers in Israel and assembled in Asia, are they any longer American products?

[9] Robert Ortner, *Voodoo Deficits*, (Homewood, Illinios: Dow Jones–Irwin, 1990), pp.142–43. In 1988 the Japanese held $285 billion U.S. in assets in the United States. "Each 1 percent decline in the dollar relative to the yen would mean a loss of nearly $3 billion to Japanese investment."

[10] Huntington, "The U.S.—Decline or Renewal," p. 82.

[11] *The New York Times* (5 February 1991), front page.

[12] *The New York Times* (8 March 1992), p. E5.

[13] Lester Thurow, "The New Economics of High Technology," *The Atlantic*, March 1992.

[14] According to the Institute of Scientific Information, there were over 1.7 million citations for American scientific papers compared with about 1.4 million for the remaining G-7 countries combined. See Chuck Freadhoff, "A New Era of Growth in U.S.?", *Investor's Business Daily*, 17 January 1992, p. 1.

[15] "Can America Compete?," *The Economist*, 18 January 1992, p. 65.

[16] What about the threat from Japan? According to Samuel P. Huntington, "Japan has neither the size, natural resources, military strength, diplomatic affiliates nor, most important , the ideological appeal to be a twentieth-century superpower." See Huntington, "The US—Decline or Renewal," p. 92.

[17] Charles R. Morris, "The Coming Global Boom," *The Atlantic*, October 1989.

[18] Paul Krugman, *The Age of Diminished Expectations* (Cambridge, Mass.: MIT Press, 1990), p. 191.

HUMAN LIFE IS PRICELESS

t is dangerous to discuss the value of a human life, or the price society should pay to save someone from dying. When it comes to the sanctity of life some would argue that economics or cost calculations have no role in the discussion, pure and simple. Human life cannot be reduced to a calculation of dollars and cents. Most believe that society should pay whatever price to save a life, or keep us in good health. If we hold that view, then we are saying that health is not like other commodities and should not be left to the vagaries of the market or just to those who can afford it. Good health care is a right we should all be entitled to regardless of income or ability to pay. To do otherwise would be a sacrilege. That's the reason why we value our universal health care programs.

Even if we believe that the avoidance of "pain and suffering" are of paramount importance in a society that values human life and human welfare, that does not mean that economics has no role to play in deciding some fundamental questions. In a world of scarce resources, even in health care, the notion of a human life being priceless has little meaning. We could allocate the entire government budget to health care trying to keep the terminally ill alive and performing expensive surgery on elderly patients. Regardless of how much money is spent, we all travel down the same road give or take a few years. But the title of this chapter begs the question, whose life are we talking about? Should society spend $500,000 on a liver transplant for someone over sixty-five and terminally ill, or allocate those funds to a rehabilitation program for young drug abusers that is sure to save some lives?[1]

The key here is that society is often confronted with the dilemma of saving a known life, such as that of a little girl who desperately needs a bone marrow transplant, or a statistical life, saved because a community spent money on highway guard rails to reduce the probability of an accident. It is only human to have more concern for someone we see suffering rather than some mathematical notion of diminishing the chances of someone dying in the future.

Let's take this idea of probability a little further. Suppose a recreational sailor goes missing at sea. How long should the coast guard keep searching knowing that the probability of finding the sailor alive diminishes as each day passes? Some would say we must keep looking until he's found. But what if that means exhausting the coast guard's limited budget for the entire year, putting future sailors at risk? What about an individual's responsibility for protecting his or her own life? Should society provide blanket health care even to people who increase their chances of illness by poor diets, drinking, smoking or undertaking dangerous activities in which they put themselves at risk? Although different from other economic goods, health and health care challenge society with the same dilemma as other economic issues: choices and consequences.

"A BUILT BED IS A FILLED BED"

One of the reasons the issue of health and how much to spend on it is so difficult to grapple with is the very notion of health itself. What does it mean to be healthy? The closer you get to the notion of health, the more elusive it becomes. It has often been said that people are only as sick as the system allows them to be. In other words, hospital use is determined not so much by the needs of the population but by the available facilities.[2] If the supply of medical facilities is expanded, it seems that doctors will find a way to use it. Therefore, "a built bed is a filled bed." For those who need evidence, consider that surgeons in the United States find twice as many patients need operations as their British counterparts.[3] Sickness is a concept that can be expanded infinitely by both the patient and the medical profession. Simply overemphasizing needs makes us needier. Free medical care also acts as an incentive to seek medical attention when it would not normally be sought. Furthermore doctors know that medicine is an uncertain science: hence (more often than not) excessive testing will be done on patients. It appears to be true that the more facilities and technology available to the medical profession, the greater the need. With universal health care coverage as we have in Canada, there is little incentive for patients to ration a service that is effectively free. In all fairness, it should also be noted that doctors are compelled to run more tests than are necessary for fear of malpractice suits, the result also being too many expensive and useless tests. Under these circumstances there can never really be enough hospital beds. For medical care, supply really does create its own demand.

HOW MUCH IS ENOUGH?

If the system is not capable of deciding how much medical treatment is enough, it is left to external rules to limit a system where costs are going up. In 1960 Canada spent about 5.5 percent of its GDP on health care. Today we are spending close to $71 billion on trying to stay healthy, which is about 8.7 percent of GDP or about $1,700 per capita (Figure 25.2). Canada spends more on health than any industrialized nation after the United States, which allocates 11.8 percent of its GNP to health spending. Health care is now our biggest single social program, and by international standards, ours is fairly expensive. It is true that we have been successful in containing any cost explosion (contrary to what the media would have us believe) but health care is expensive and can easily get out of hand if not held in check.[4] One only has to look south of the border to see what can happen.

With all these health care dollars, are we a healthier people? On the basis of life expectancy and infant mortality rates, Canadians are not the healthiest, nor are the Americans. The British have a life expectancy as good as the Americans — they spent two-thirds less per capita on health care[5] during the 1980s but lived on average the same number of years. The Japanese are the real winners — they spend only 6.7 percent of their GDP on health care but live longer than anyone. Many objective observers describe the Japanese system as outmoded, and note that they don't seem to believe in surgery at all.[6] The Japanese may be on to something. Epidemiological studies measuring unnecessary care in medical procedures suggest that between 20 and 50 percent of surgical and other medical interventions did not prolong life or reduce the incidence of death.[7] And some procedures do us more harm than good.[8]

	Life expectancy at birth (years)		Infant Mortality per 1,000 live births	Health spending as a % of GDP	Doctors per 10,000 population
	Male	Female		($ per capita)	
Canada	73.0	79.8	7.2	8.7 (1,683)	22
Japan	75.9	81.8	4.6	6.7 (1,035)	16
Britain	72.4	78.1	8.4	5.8 (836)	14
France	72.4	80.6	7.5	8.7 (1,274)	30
West Germany	71.8	78.4	7.5	8.2 (1,232)	30
U.S.	71.5	78.5	9.7	11.8 (2,354)	23

Source: The Economist (6 July 1991), p. 5; and OECD.

TABLE 25.1 HEALTH INDICATORS, 1989

GETTING THE MOST FROM OUR DOLLAR

Nothing so far is meant to argue that the concept of medical care has no meaning or that good health is simply subjective. The seriously ill *should* get priority and special claim on limited medical services. The question now is, how do we continue to deliver the highest level of health care to all Canadians given that most provinces are either explicitly or implicitly putting a cap on health spending? One way is to impose some form of user fee. Studies show that even a modest increase in fees can deter doctor visits.[9] Given the sanctity of universal health care in Canada, user fees are probably politically unacceptable in reducing health care costs.

A more likely area of realizing potential savings is rationing certain medical procedures. One way is to study which medical procedures work, and which don't and perhaps get away from the notion of "anything and everything for the patient" regardless of what it costs. Doctors should be asked to order extra tests, or perform surgery only if the benefits or outcome have some reasonable chance of success. Doctors will want to use scarce resources where the marginal benefit of doing so is equal to or greater than the marginal cost. For example, because heart disease is one of the biggest killers of adults in Canada, some would automatically argue that more money should go to fight that illness. But if the chances or probability of successfully eradicating liver illness, which doesn't kill as many people, are better, then money would be more effectively spent on liver disorders than on heart disease because more lives could be saved. The notion of opportunity cost for health does not have the same impact as other goods we desire. If we want more cars, we have to give up ever-increasing amounts of, say, textiles. In the end we'll have more cars, but less clothing. This is not so with health care. We may give up more of everything else, but we may not necessarily get better health. In a real sense health care is a unique product where sacrificing other goods may bring no positive benefits unless you enjoy medical treatment for its own good.[10] That is why hard choices have to be made in cutting down on needlessly expensive medical procedures.

For those who may find rationing of medical services distasteful, it should be noted that we already implicitly ration or allocate medical services given that people have to wait months for elective surgery and other diagnostic procedures, and doctors may decide to do no more for a dying older patient. To be cost effective, rationing should not be based on first-come first-served basis but on a priority of need and probability of success. The Health Services Commission in Oregon is doing just that. In the Oregon Experiment all medical visits are ranked according to the costs and benefits by consulting with health care workers. Funds are then applied to medical procedures on a priority list. A major criticism of the Oregon plan is that it only rations for the poor because the rich can buy whatever medical procedure they want. One way around the problem is to assess the benefits of medical procedures. One researcher came up with a measurable concept of quality-adjusted life years to evaluate the effectiveness of various operations.

Is human life priceless? In a moral sense, yes. From an economic point of view, however, even if society decides to put more resources into health care (which implies that other priorities and sectors of the community such as education or law enforcement have to go with less), the fact remains that more money does not guarantee better health or that we will live longer. The health sciences can only do so much. Technology is no savior. Evidence is accumulating that even high-tech isn't the answer, and that medical equipment is being overused with dubious results regarding diagnosis. The next decade will most likely see a growing shift in emphasis from illness cure to illness care. But to continue under the assumption that life should be prolonged at all costs is economic folly in a world of scarce resources. Health care is like any other commodity — the more we want it, the more we have to give up to get it but without the guarantee that we'll be better off. Even regarding questions of life and death, we cannot escape the realities and constraints of economic costs and benefits.

NOTES

1 In the United States, for example, 30 percent of Medicare's budget goes to patients in their last year of life. It is common place for coronary by-passes to be performed on patients in their sixties and seventies. Even expensive heart transplants are performed on patients in their sixties. By contrast, the Japanese offer no organ transplants, and in Britain, the National Health Service doesn't generally provide kidney dialysis for people over fifty-five.

2 Medical technology itself determines where health resources are allocated. For example, electronic fetal monitoring is done on three-quarters of all births in Canada with no evidence that it does any good on birth outcomes. Source: See Robert Evans, "Health Care: Is the System Sick?," *Canada at Risk? Canadian Public Policies in the 1990s* (C.D. Howe Institute, 1991).

3 Steven E. Rhoads, *The Economist's View of the World, Government, Markets and Public Policy* (Cambridge, England: Cambridge University Press, 1985), pp. 29–30.

4 One of the reasons for higher medical costs is rising hospital care. Productivity, or output per worker, can usually be raised with investment in capital equipment. Hospitals went from being labour intensive institutions in the 1950s to highly capital intensive today without the benefits of high productivity. But with expensive machinery and technology, such as blood and tissue analyzers, body scanners, and nuclear magnetic imagers, more knowledge intensive workers were required. Hospitals became more capital intensive and needed more highly skilled, and highly paid workers to go with the technology. Modern hospitals have become "labour and capital intensive monstrosities": See Peter Drucker, "The New Productivity Challenge," *Harvard Business Review*, November–December, 1991, pp. 69–79. Hospitals are by far the greatest users of our health care dollars taking 59.2 percent of all health care funding in Canada in 1985 followed by 19.7 going to doctors, 13.2 percent to drugs and prostheses, and the remaining 8.0 percent to all other health expenditures.

5 British men live 71.34 years compared with 71.00 years for Americans, while American women had a slight edge, living 78.30 years compared to 77.35 for British women. However, the Americans spend about three times per capita more on health care than the British.

6 Robert Evans, *Canada at Risk?*, p. 234.

7 Malcolm C. Brown, *Health Economics and Policy* (Toronto: McClelland & Stewart,1991), p. 67.

[8] One classic example of bad surgery was uncovered by Dr. John Wennberg of Dartmouth Medical School who found that prostatectomy operations (the removal of enlarged prostrate glands) do not improve quality of life and actually reduce life expectancy. Martin Barkin, Ontario's former deputy minister of health, has done similar studies on cardiac surgery. See *The Economist*, 6 July 1991.

[9] However, money is not the only deterring factor. One study, found that taking longer to get to a clinic reduces patient use. Hospital emergency wards are usually quiet on evenings when there is a major event on TV. Any small impediment, it seems, reduces clinic visits. Steven E. Rhoads, *The Economist's View of the World* (Cambridge, England: Cambridge University Press, 1985), p. 29.

[10] Generally people don't demand medical care for its own good. Going to the doctor is not a pleasant experience, unless you suffer from a condition know as Munchausen's Sydrome and want the attention of medical staff. What most of us want when we're sick is to get well — fast. This gives people unrealistic expectations of what modern medicine can deliver.

MYTH 26

ECONOMISTS ALWAYS DISAGREE

conomics always makes the headlines, especially if the news is bad. A day does not go by without some economic news and questions about how the economy is doing: Are we in a recession? What are interest rates doing? What are we going to do about unemployment? Why are prices rising (or falling)? Is free trade with Mexico good or bad? The questions are endless and all the while economists are asked to give quick and easy answers to tough questions. But when their answers begin with the words "It depends ...," people's eyes glaze over and they start writing off the profession as arcane, theoretical, academic, obscure, and most of all, irrelevant. Economists are seen as quasi-professionals who live in their own world, building models with unrealistic assumptions that produce answers so full of qualifications that they are meaningless. There is also a widespread perception that economics as a subject cannot be trusted because economists never agree on anything or, in other words, that "if you lined up every economist from end to end, they still wouldn't reach a conclusion." But *is* there widespread disagreement among economists?

MICROECONOMICS VS. MACROECONOMICS

Before trying to sort out whether or not economists "always" disagree, it is important to understand that economics has two main areas of study. The first is commonly known as microeconomics, and deals mainly with issues about how individual consumers make decisions to get the most satisfaction from the goods they purchase given a limited income, and how firms can get the highest return on their investments. It's called "micro" because it deals with the behaviour of individual agents in the economy. More generally, this area of economics looks at how prices and production of goods and services are determined in free markets. Anything that has to do with price distortion in the free market (exchange rates, tariffs, minimum wages, rent controls, and pollution taxes) would be considered within the realm of microeconomics. Economic theory says that the fewer impediments, or government interference, to the adjustments of market "prices," the more efficient the overall economy will be.

The second major area of economic study is known as macroeconomics, which deals mainly with broad issues concerning employment, inflation, balance of payments, national debts and deficits, taxation, money supply and interest rates. Where microeconomics deals essentially with questions of efficiency, and how best to use society's resources, macroeconomics is predominantly about questions of *equity*, in other words the distribution of income and how best to achieve the objectives of full employment, price stability, and the elimination of poverty.

WHAT CAN BE DONE VS. WHAT OUGHT TO BE DONE

In both micro- and macroeconomics there are two further distinctions: things that people feel *can* be done, called positive economics, and things that people feel *ought* to be done, called normative economics. Economics, like any science, is concerned with propositions and questions that can be shown to be false or true by appealing to the facts and actual observations. These are issues that deal with positive statements such as, "Lower taxes will decrease employment," "Free trade with Mexico will increase trade and lower prices," or "Rent control will provide more affordable housing for the poor." These statements can be tested and resolved by appealing to facts and analyzing data. Normative attitudes such as "Society should spend more money on health care than on education" or "We ought to build more shelters for the homeless" cannot be resolved by appealing to facts because they deal with values and value judgments. That is not to say that these matters are unimportant or that economists cannot have opinions of what *should be* rather than what *can be*, only that it has to be understood that there are limits to what economics can say regarding issues of value. When an economist is asked if we should subsidize more public education, it is a value judgment that has to be made. These are things decided by society and not the market. Where economists can contribute is in helping to select the most efficient programs for society to reach its educational goals, or in other words, giving advice on where to allocate its resources.

In terms of whether or not economists agree or disagree, there was a survey of economists in business, government, and universities in which they were asked to comment on thirty propositions to find out if there was indeed substantial disagreement over certain issues.[1] Contrary to conventional wisdom, the result was that there is considerable agreement among economists regarding questions in microeconomics about the market and the price system (see Table 26.1). For example, 81 percent of the economists surveyed agreed that tariffs and import quotas reduce economic welfare. Economists, therefore, believe that removing barriers to trade would be beneficial. There's also considerable agreement on questions about rent control, minimum wages, wage and price controls and the use of taxes over regulations to control pollution. The reason for agreement is mainly that there exist data and analysis to support the statements. Positive statements can usually be resolved by research and investigation.[2]

Of the thirty propositions covering macro and micro issues, there was significant consensus regarding twenty of them. The study found that the greatest amount of disagreement among economists was with macro issues that dealt with normative rather than posi-

Proposition	Generally Agree	Agree with Provisions	Generally Disagree
Tariffs and import quotas reduce general economic welfare.	81	16	3
A minimum wage increases unemployment among young and unskilled workers.	68	22	10
Wage and price controls should be used to control inflation.	6	22	72
A ceiling on rents reduces the quantity and quality of housing available.	78	20	2
Effluent taxes represent a better approach to pollution control than imposition of pollution ceilings.	50	31	19

Source: Adapted from J.R. Kearl *et al.* "A Confusion of Economists?", *American Economic Review*, vol. 69, no. 2., May 1979.

TABLE 26.1 WHERE ECONOMISTS DO AGREE (%)

tive questions. For example, economists disagreed about whether governments should act as an employer of last resort and initiate guaranteed job programs or what the size of the government should be.

PERCEPTION VS. REALITY

If there is so much that economists agree on, why does the myth persist that the profession cannot come to some concensus? There are a number of reasons for the perception that economists are in disagreement. To begin with, economics isn't always easy to understand and is often confusing for the layperson who is not familiar with how economists are trained. The case of inflation is a good example. When an expert from Statistics Canada says that prices are down, even though all around us we see them going up, the economist is usually talking about the rate of change in an index for all prices from one period over another (e.g., now compared to last month or last year). There is no disagreement or confusion, just a matter of which benchmark is being used. Then there are differences between the impact of government policy in the short and long term, which can be confusing. A cut in taxes may increase consumer buying in the short term, but investment and consumption of capital goods will be affected in the long run.

Where there *is* fundamental disagreement among economists is not on problems of measurement but on issues about values. Support for the arts is a case in point. A more politically conservative economist might argue that governments have no business spending our tax dollars on public television, or on building ballet and opera houses, because only a small group of people will end up using them. If some people want more arts, this economist would argue, they should pay for it themselves. However, those defending such spending might accuse those who argue against support for the arts of being "philistines" and make the case that society overall is enriched by the arts. In this type of dichotomy, which course should be taken by the government? In a democracy, that's a question for the electorate (not the economists) to decide.[3]

As in any profession, economists are not politically unbiased. This does not mean that they disagree on the impact of government policies and programs, but rather on the proper role of government and its obligation to income distribution and support for certain income groups. On issues that are dominated by values and politics, intelligent people can simply "agree to disagree." But aside from all this, there is another reason why economists seem to disagree and that is that the media demands it. If there's a controversy of any kind, the media wants to get *both* sides of the story even if the majority of experts believe only one of them. This is exactly what occurred during the great free trade debate before Canada signed an agreement with the United States. It didn't make any difference whether the majority of economists believed that lowering tariffs would be of benefit to the country. Someone could always be found to take the opposite position. This gave the misleading impression that economists were divided on such a fundamental issue, and consequently that their advice on other policy issues was probably of little value as well. That is the misfortune of a superficial perception of economists by the layperson because there exists a considerable amount of agreement among economists on substantive issues. Economists do differ on issues of normative macroeconomics where ideology plays a big role. That is exactly where there is the greatest disagreement among economists, and the area of most media attention.[4]

The media seems obsessed with short-term forecasting. They ask questions, such as "Will we have a recession next year?" and "What will the discount interest rate be next July?" The media want answers to meet deadlines from experts who are not trained to forecast like weather reporters do. Economic analysis and reasoning may be sound, but as with any discipline where all contingencies (both economic and political) cannot be foreseen, prediction is a precarious game at best. But predictions are what the media wants, not qualifications. Economists only end up looking foolish if they equivocate when confronted with "simple" questions that are impossible to answer.[5]

Of course there are real disagreements among economists on a wide range of issues that involve recent events that are not yet well understood, where there is still research to be done and data to be gathered. But that exists in any science or profession. It is wrong to think that there's more controversy now or that economics can make less of a contribution to public policy because economists "never seem to agree on anything."

NOTES

[1] J.R. Kearl *et al.* " A Confusion of Economists?" *American Economic Review*, vol. 69, no. 2, May 1979.

[2] Not all positive statements or propositions can be resolved by research or facts. "Elvis lives and was last seen in Kansas" is a positive statement, but no amount of evidence proving Elvis is dead will convince everyone who believes Elvis is still alive.

[3] It would be a cruel government indeed that allowed everything to be determined by the market. Even smokers and drug addicts generally support policies that discourage smoking and drugs.

[4] It is in macroeconomic issues where the profession is deeply divided. The split between the Keynesians and monetarists is a long-standing feud, though Keynesianism was the predominant school through the 1960s and 1970s. Now there are supply siders, rational expectationists, and post-Keynesians. The average newspaper reader no more understands the differences than he understands the differences in the rival factions of the PLO.

[5] Economists are faulted for their inability to predict recessions, exchange and interest rate movement, and the impact of monetary and fiscal policy. Forecasting using economic models is more an art than a science. It's almost impossible to predict with any degree of accuracy unless certain variables are held constant and the behaviour of consumers and companies is completely understood. The economy is too complex and changing for any model, regardless of how sophisticated, to capture all the dynamic changes in an economy. Economic models should be used as guides by policy makers rather than as instruments to predict the future.

Scientific America
Globe